# A GUIDE TO PARENTING EMOTIONALLY STRONG CHILDREN

## THE SINGLE PARENT'S GUIDE TO OVERCOMING THE CHALLENGES OF CO-PARENTING

WILLEM CUNNINGHAM

# TABLE OF CONTENTS

# INTRODUCTION: IT'S A JOURNEY

"Dad, why are you and mommy not living together anymore?"

This book is here to help you answer some difficult questions your children might ask as you start the divorce process. You and your partner have concluded that marriage is no longer working.

You are signing the papers and drafting a parenting plan, but you cannot help but wonder…

*What will happen to our children? Did I make the right decision to leave my partner? How can I help my child grow into an emotionally strong individual when I am a mess? Will my child learn to understand that this is best? How can I cultivate a loving relationship in this new family dynamic?*

**After a divorce, there will be shifts in your parent-child relationship.**

In most cases, when people get married, they do so with the expectation that their union will last for the rest of their lives. However, the fact is that divorce is a rather typical occurrence. Year after year, a significant number of marriages are dissolved for a variety of reasons. When a marriage fails, both partners must remember that they still have responsibilities to themselves and their children, even if they no longer live together.

To live up to that obligation calls for various actions and choices. Parents must first be alert to the warning signs that show their children struggle to adjust to the divorce.

Parents must adapt to and be aware of future changes in their relationships with their children. In many instances, parents must construct new parenting responsibilities for their children and then adapt to those roles.

*Beware of the red flags.*

Children who go through the trauma of their parents divorcing may display a range of behaviors and emotions, including depression, anger, confusion, a sense of being split between their two parents, feelings of guilt, and anxiety about what the future holds (Dixon, 2017).

*How can we tell when it becomes problematic?*

Action may need to be taken to address these struggles if your child shows extreme emotions, such as depression or anxiety symptoms, over an extended period, which interferes with their ability to academically or socially perform. The same may be said for children who have decided they do not want to participate in extracurricular activities, mainly if they quit doing so without providing a reason.

What can you do as a parent to help your child feel secure and stable during and after the divorce?

*Provide consistency with character to them.*

As parents, we must understand how divorce influences family dynamics. We need to adopt a strategy for prioritizing the creation of as much consistency as possible for our children. If things are rocky between you and your ex-partner and you can't seem to work together, consider hiring a mediator. Consistency in all areas is essential; this may have to do with their routines, vacations, extracurricular activities, and so on.

Because children frequently lack the skills necessary to negotiate significant life transitions, patience and empathy are just as crucial. While the wounds from the divorce are still raw, we must limit our children's exposure to new love partners out of regard for their sentiments.

*Taking on new parental responsibilities.*

Counselor and peacemaker are two new parental responsibilities that may emerge. Some parents may assume the position of counselor for their children and just listen while their children talk about how the divorce has made them feel. At the same time, one parent may need to take on the role of family mediator to establish a safe and balanced connection between their children and extended family members.

*The role of a parent lasts a lifetime.*

Getting a divorce is always complex for everyone involved in the process. Children may find the change easier, though, if their parents encourage continuity and teamwork out of concern for their best interests.

If you're feeling overwhelmed by all this information and the challenges ahead, take a deep breath and let go. Not to sound cliche, but it's going to be okay.

**How will this book help me?**

This book is here to guide you on this journey. It provides divorced or separated parents with information on how to co-parent their children successfully.

The goal is for you to feel a sense of relief, knowing that the skills you provide your children today will help them become mature and emotionally strong individuals.

Welcome to the most diverse, complex, and rewarding journey, you'll ever encounter to co-parent successfully.

# SECTION 1: THE PROCESS OF CO-PARENTING

The purpose of this section is to provide you with a road map for getting through the divorce process, some strategies for coping with stress, and a brief introduction to the basics of co-parenting and why the divorce might benefit your children.

# CHAPTER 1: NAVIGATING THROUGH THE SEPARATION PROCESS

This would be an excellent place to start if you're new to co-parenting or just need guidance on the process. This chapter explores how the divorce process unfolds, how to work through complex and unwanted emotions, what a parenting plan is, and why you need one.

## THE DIVORCE

When a couple decides to end their marriage, they often face financial, emotional, and legal problems, especially when children are involved. Parents who are getting divorced and have kids have to figure out things like who gets the kids and how much money should go to each parent.

To end your marriage and continue with your life while also protecting your children's best interests, this guidance for divorcing with children will help you prepare for what to expect.

## Marriage Dissolution

Following the submission of a request for divorce, the required divorce paperwork must be delivered to your partner in accordance with the laws of your country. This may require payment to the sheriff or a private process server to have your partner's legal documents served.

Then, your partner has a certain amount of time to answer. They can disagree with the factual data in your court documents, agree with them, or file their complaint.

After this response, the court case will start. In a simple, uncontested divorce, this could involve a short hearing. Another option is to go to trial. Both parties can submit witnesses and evidence to support their desired custody, support, and property distribution arrangements.

A court appearance will be necessary if children are involved—even in an uncontested divorce. In relatively straightforward divorce cases, some courts will allow a judgment to be rendered based solely on the pleadings submitted by the parties. However, this strategy is typically not used in more complicated circumstances, such as when questions concerning child support and custody must be resolved.

## Is It Possible to Have Children and Have an Uncontested Divorce?

An uncontested divorce is the least complicated and inexpensive way to end a marriage. You avoid wasting time and money on trial by reaching a mutually agreeable settlement with your partner.

Generally, getting a divorce without fighting is possible and even encouraged if you have children. Unfortunately, this implies that you and your partner must reach a consensus on every subject that will be part of the divorce settlement.

Those things are:

- How will physical custody be split?
- How will custody rights be split (who will make decisions affecting the children)?
- Where will the parents' and children's homes be?
- How and when will child support be paid?
- How will the property from the marriage be split?
- Whether or not there will be alimony.

If you can't agree on these things on your own, you can do so with the help of a mediator.

Your attorney will also be able to explain your state's relevant child custody, support, and other laws. So, you can protect your own and your child's interests by making choices based on what you know.

### How to Decide Who Gets the Children

It depends on your child's needs and what's best for them at that time.

Parenting plans allow you and your partner to outline the details of sharing custody, including physical and legal custody aspects. Where a child resides is known as "physical custody." In contrast, the parent with legal custody is the one who makes decisions for them, such as what school they should attend or what kind of medical care is best.

The court will decide if you can't agree on how to share

custody. In most cases, courts favor maintaining contact between the parents and consider a variety of variables, such as who has served as the child's primary caretaker, how stable a home each parent can provide, and the child's needs.

## Guidelines for a Child-Friendly Divorce

Divorcing when you have children can be challenging, but you can do things to make it easier.

Here are some ideas that might help:

### Keep the Children Out of the Divorce Process

Most of the time, children shouldn't be at divorce hearings, and you shouldn't tell them too much about what's happening. Children may be traumatized if they witness their parents arguing in court, especially if there are accusations of adultery or violence.

### Don't Talk Badly About the Other Parent

The effects of parental alienation are far-reaching and long-lasting. It can also change the way the court decides who gets custody. Parents should try not to say bad things about each other in front of their children or complain about each other.

### Plan for the Future

It's important to consider what your children will need in the long run. Even if your children are still relatively young, consider including a provision in the divorce settlement agreement that addresses how college costs would be split between you and your ex-partner.

### Finding Legal Representation amid a Family Law Case

An experienced divorce attorney can help with issues like child custody and maintenance, which are governed by state law, and your attorney can clarify the specifics. You can increase the likelihood of the outcomes you want as your marriage ends with the support of your attorney, who can assist you in settlement negotiations or courtroom arguments.

## THE CHANGE PROCESS

Divorce may drastically alter your role in the family and as a parent, or it may keep it mostly the same. Maintaining familiar routines and relationships throughout and after a divorce might help children adjust more swiftly. Yet it's conceivable that won't be an option. When a family is reorganized, one or both parents may have to take on responsibilities previously held by the other—homework help, cooking, and transportation.

It's also possible that parents will wish to play a more active part in raising the child than they did throughout the marriage. Adopting a new schedule and setting new expectations can be challenging for parents and children, even if the change is beneficial.

For example, a parent who has previously deferred to their partner in matters of discipline could suddenly want to weigh in on issues like whether their child should attend a sleepover at a friend's house or how to handle sibling conflict. When it comes to their children's schedules, a parent who previously delegated that responsibility to their partner would prefer to spend more time with their children from now on.

Divorce can be difficult, but it might help to have a basic understanding of how relationships shift. When people reflect on their past relationships, they often go through a process of *revision,* focusing on the negative aspects of their past partner. They can't help but dwell on how their ex let them down and only recall the negative aspects of their relationship. This is a natural and often beneficial occurrence. It can aid in *getting over* the other person and ending a toxic relationship.

This is a common experience for both parties, regardless of who files for divorce. But many can't move past how their partner has let them down. During this time, we must remember that being an *awful* partner is different from being an *awful* parent.

It's not uncommon for relationships to end unexpectedly and without any explanation. In certain partnerships, one or both partners may begin contemplating or even discussing a breakup years before it occurs. Divorces are seldom easy, but there is one constant: people don't heal similarly. Everyone goes through their healing process in their own time.

## How to Handle Change

Change can be good if we let it take its course and embrace the journey with open arms. Keep an open mindset as you navigate the new waters of change.

*Life is ten percent what you make it and ninety percent how you take it.* – Ben Franklin

Embracing rather than resisting change can have positive outcomes, helping us learn and grow. It lets us grow and gives us chances we wouldn't have otherwise.

Every person has a different tolerance for change; some adapt quickly, while others resist it tooth and nail. If you struggle to adjust to new circumstances, here is a list of things you can do to feel renewed and in control.

How to handle change better (*6 Ways to Improve How You Navigate Change*, 2022):

### Manage Your Expectations

Be honest with yourself about what you're getting into. You can only expect to try something new or learn something new and be good at it after dedicating time and effort to it. Expectations are a valuable tool for helping individuals set objectives; just be careful not to put too much pressure on yourself.

### Acknowledge That Change Is a Part of Life

Change is always going to happen. You must accept the possibility that the situation will shift or your expectations will be hindered. When you accept change, you don't try to stop it from happening.

It's okay if things don't work out exactly as you hoped. Accepting the way things are can help you deal well with change. It enables you to adapt, accept the transition, and move on.

### Change Is a Lesson

If you can learn to accept change, you can start learning from everything you do. If you are willing to learn, change can teach you a lot. Recall a time when you were resistant to change and think about why you felt that way. In retrospect, you'll see its value or learn something from it.

## RESTRUCTURING THE FAMILY

When a couple gets divorced or separated, their family structure changes significantly. The structure that a family used to know as *normal* changes into something unfamiliar, but unfamiliar doesn't mean it's *bad*.

It can be difficult for everyone, even children, to move ahead during this period due to the intensity of their emotions. Parents need to deal with their emotional difficulties to be strong role models for their children and help them overcome obstacles in life.

Even though all of this is easy to say, it can be challenging for co-parents and families to return to a normal routine. Reorganizing your family following a breakup, rather than trying to go back to how things were, may give everyone a fresh start and a renewed sense of purpose.

Whether you've just divorced or have been separated for a while, it's essential to think about these obstacles and how to reorganize your family positively.

The way forward:

## Moving and Creating New Routines

No matter how you look at it, moving your family after a divorce is hard. Whether one or both of you are relocating, your child's daily routine and schedule may be entirely disrupted.

Everyone in the household may experience feelings of alienation and unease after relocating. Despite their natural ability to adjust well to unfamiliar circumstances, children require more help as you reorganize your family's home and routines.

Consider the long-term effects of a move on the children if you or your ex-partner (or both of you) have to make one after the divorce. Children can feel lost and confused when they have to move from either one of their homes.

Try to make a move into a new house as easy as possible. If you are moving, it may be time to reorganize your living situation to make the most of your new surroundings. Consider what you already own, what you still require, and what you can do without. If you're buying or renovating a new house, encourage your children to participate in building your home so they can feel as though they have some control over the layout of your new residence.

Just as you need to reorganize your new home, you need to

reorganize your family's routine into a schedule that works for you as a parent. Your schedule should be based on what your children need most. You must do everything you can to ensure your children can keep as much of their previous schedule as possible, such as participating in extracurricular activities and spending time with friends.

## Holidays and Other Special Events

After a divorce, navigating through the first few holidays and other important family occasions will be challenging. There's no denying the feelings that go along with these dates. When you are celebrating these well-known events in a setting that is foreign to you or with a group of people who are not like you, it might seem weird and awkward.

When children witness long-standing family rituals, it might be difficult for them to split their time with their parents on a day that holds special meaning for them.

It's better to make new traditions than to attempt to keep doing things the same way every year. Think about the values important to you in your old holiday traditions and work those into your new ideal.

Early on, you and your co-parent should discuss and select how you will participate in the holiday celebrations with your children. If you want to avoid problems a few months later, make sure your new plans are written down and on the calendar as soon as possible.

## Objectives and Top Concerns

A divorce can make you think about many things, including how you raise your children. This is because your parenting styles will change as a co-parent compared to when you were a unit.

Have a strategy before you face a challenge, such as deciding how to divide the expense of extracurricular activities or what to do in an emergency. Try rearranging your parenting objectives to fit in with your new family schedule.

Your fundamental beliefs about parenting won't shift, but how you put those beliefs into practice could need some reorganizing. Think about the qualities you want to preserve about your family and try to incorporate as many of them as possible.

As for the objectives, decide on co-parenting priorities that work for your new family. As you set your goals, think about your children and what would benefit them in the long run.

You need to accept the new circumstances in which your household now finds itself and devise a strategy to make the best of them. Always look ahead so that you can figure out how to make your new family dynamic work for everyone.

## LIFE AFTER THE DIVORCE

Your future feels unknown after a divorce. How would your life be without your partner? Will you find another person? Will you become lonely? Continuing in an unpleasant relationship frequently seems worse than these uncertainties.

It might be hard to move on after a divorce, but it's crucial to realize that it might have been necessary. Be kind to yourself, and remember that healing takes time. The recovery process after a divorce may take two or three years, as each individual's recovery process is unique.

Grief is a normal response to loss; getting divorced results in several losses. The loss of friends and shared experiences; the loss of any kind of assistance, including financial, intellectual, social, and emotional support; and the loss of shared aspirations and goals.

## The Stages

You will go through five fundamental emotional stages during your divorce. These are extremely similar to the five stages of grieving, and if you want to heal, you must go through them.

Here are the five emotional phases you experience:

### 1. Denial

Denial is the initial stage of refusing to acknowledge the truth of the divorce. It is a natural protection that gives you time to acknowledge what is happening. During this early period, things will seem surreal. You could assume that it's a misunderstanding or a bluff, and you won't be able to accept what's occurring. Most of the time, we deceive ourselves into believing that it's only a temporary rough patch and that our partner will soon regain his or her senses.

### 2. Anger

Emotions begin to simmer as soon as reality settles in. Perhaps you are upset about being let down. Finding a healthy outlet for your rage is crucial to the healing process. Anger during a divorce is common; the trick lies in handling your anger. If you are a parent, remember that your actions are an example for your children to follow. Different types of anger can appear, including brief wrath, simmering resentment, and prolonged bitterness. It may be hard to think properly when angry; anger can be harmful and self-defeating, but you can only heal if you let go of it.

3. **Negotiation**

After the anger subsides, a period of profound uncertainty and fright takes place. When you reach this stage, you negotiate and try to have problems fixed that are beyond your control. It is reconsidering your choice to be divorced. "If only I had done such and such" is one of the things you may say. You may feel guilty and blame yourself for what happened.

4. **Depression**

Depression happens when the loss brought on by the divorce sinks in. You could doubt your capacity for coping with grief and use unhealthy coping mechanisms to dull your suffering, such as binge eating, sleeping too little, drinking too much alcohol, etc. Instead, you should take care of yourself and discover constructive means of getting over your melancholy.

5. **Acknowledgment**

The last step is acceptance. No longer a danger, change may even be welcomed. You could be more tolerant of your new situation and more upbeat about the future, depending on your circumstances. You have, in any event, made it through and endured a trying moment. Life has shifted, and you can finally see the bright new horizon.

### Feel All the Emotions

You and your partner can go through various emotional stages simultaneously or go through the stages in a different sequence. The most important thing is that you go through and endure each one.

Various contradictory feelings, such as rage, resentment, fear, grief, relief, and uncertainty, are acceptable. Recognize and accept these emotions. Although they will hurt, attempting to ignore or repress them will only prolong the mourning process. Feel these emotions, but try not to focus on the bad or overthink the matter. Spending too much time on negative emotions like blame, resentment, and anger depletes your energy. It keeps you from moving on to better things.

### When You Move On

When you commit to someone, you build several aspirations and goals. Letting these aspirations go as you decide on a separation might be hard. Be heartened by the knowledge that new aspirations and ambitions will ultimately take the place of your previous ones. At the same time, you mourn the loss of the future you previously anticipated.

Even if you wanted a divorce, mourning the life and way of living you have lost is expected when a marriage ends. After a breakup, grief has the power to render you helpless, but eventually, the anguish starts to fade.

You'll begin to live again, little by little, day by day. However, if you don't sense any forward motion, it's possible that you're depressed. When you can't stand being by yourself, friends who will let you cry on their shoulders and sleep on their sofa are priceless. However, it is usually preferable to speak with a therapist to jump-start your new life. Similarly, creating a support network for oneself is among the most crucial actions you can take.

Support during this time is essential, so speak with reliable friends and relatives to help you grieve. Count on your close friends to stop you from acting irrationally, such as by bothering your ex's new partner or contacting him or her late at night after a few drinks of wine. Those who have gone through traumatic divorces may be of considerable assistance, as they are familiar with the situation and might help you recover. Spend time with individuals who are upbeat and with whom you can communicate without fear of being criticized, judged, or told what to do.

This is a time for you to connect with your individuality since "we" no longer exist. Attempt to meet new people if you believe the divorce caused you to lose your social network. You could also feel alone in a world of couples after your divorce; you are now swimming in a different social pool, and your married friends might want to avoid hanging out with you more frequently than they did in the past. Surround yourself with individuals who share your interests.

## WHAT IS A PARENTING PLAN?

Divorce starts as a win-lose situation. One parent may appear wealthy, while the other struggles to make ends meet. On the other hand, the parent who appears to have it all spends little time with their children, whereas the other parent gives them all the attention in the world.

Regardless of whether or not this particular example applies to your circumstances, the key to developing the ideal parenting strategy for your family is to strike a balance between the demands of family life, your child's priorities, your feelings, and everything else in between. The optimal parenting plan considers schedules, holidays, finances, and communication.

### Make a Parenting Plan

These six steps can help any parent create the optimal one. Your scenario may require extra steps.

Here's how to get started:

#### Step 1: Know Your Children's Needs

The optimal parenting strategy puts your child first. Their best interests include physical and emotional requirements. You may know your child's best interests, but examining them can help you develop a *map* of the perfect parenting strategy.

Your family's parenting plan must be customized. Consider their physical and emotional requirements when making a plan for your child.

Physical requirements include housing, food, clothes, movement, exercise, rest, medical treatment, protection from injury, etc. Emotional requirements include mental health, parent connections, temperament, etc.

Some parents consider their child's desires when determining their best interests. Their wishes generally depend on their age and growth.

The following are some examples of other issues that may play a direct role in determining whether or not your parenting plan is in the best interests of your child:

- **Distance between residences**: Distance from each residence to school, extracurriculars, friends, and other key destinations.
- **Parental work schedules**: When creating a parenting plan, these are only a few considerations for your child's best interests. Cover any family- or child-specific matters.

### Step 2: Pick a Good Parenting Schedule

The schedule will set your family's new schedule and show how much time the child will spend with each parent. Identifying and keeping a family-friendly schedule as part of your parenting strategy is crucial.

Based on your child's needs and co-parenting, numerous methods exist to structure a parenting plan and choose a routine. Your parenting schedule can alter as your child grows to fit their requirements. Younger children may benefit from frequent visits with both parents. However, older children may prefer fewer changes.

Many family courts advise parents to share parenting time 50/50.

The 50/50 parenting schedules work for many families, but not all. Alternating visits on the weekends and throughout the week is an option that may be viable for individuals who are required to adhere to a varied schedule. However, if one parent doesn't live close enough for frequent visits, consider arranging for your child to spend a longer time with that parent, perhaps over the summer or winter holidays.

Include holidays and birthdays in your parenting routine; having a plan in place will simplify these dates.

### Step 3: Plan Communication

As you become more comfortable with your new shared parenting routine, it is reasonable to believe that you will figure out the most effective way to maintain communication with your children and your co-parent.

When your children begin living in both your and your partner's homes, you may find yourself wishing for a more formalized method of communicating your child's most vital information back and forth between the two locations.

Make communication decisions now.

Make a plan with your co-parent to keep in touch and exchange information about your child—video messaging or regular phone calls can help you stay in contact with your children.

### Step 4: Plan for Major Choices and Legal Custody

You and the co-parent maintain legal custody of your children; you should devise a strategy for how the two of you will make joint choices on the many aspects of your children's upbringing.

Over time, you'll make decisions concerning your child's education, health, religion, and culture. Be sure to document your early decisions and establish a communication strategy in your parenting plan.

Prepare for emergency decisions. Though you want to avoid being in a scenario where you have to make a hasty choice, such as after an injury, it's preferable to be prepared.

### Step 5: Assess Your Child's Financial Situation

Parents share financial responsibility for their children regardless of legal and physical custody. If one parent earns more than the other, child support may be required to pay for basic living expenses and luxuries.

You need to clarify your child support payments. To track child-related spending, keep a log of all the ongoing expenses and possible ones in the near future. Even if child support paid most of those expenditures, this information could assist each parent in realizing what they are spending on their child. This information can assist parents with their budgets—plan for expenditures beyond child support. Know how you will distribute responsibility for these things and use a secure means of issuing refunds when needed.

Even if the steps discussed here cover a big part of the factors separating parents need to consider when crafting the ideal parenting plan, you should still be prepared to handle any other concerns unique to your circumstance. If you want personalized advice on your parenting plan, go to your lawyer or other legal professionals.

### Step 6: Maintain Your Goals

As soon as your parenting plan has been formulated and implemented, it is essential to start thinking about particular goals that will assist in making your ideal plan a success both now and in the future.

*Imagine how you'd like your child to remember this moment.*

Even though there may be some difficult moments as everyone adjusts to their new family dynamic, do everything you can to leave your child with happy memories.

Your parenting plan is not a competition or a test of who is better suited to raise your child. Instead, co-parenting should be flexible and cooperative.

### Going Forward

Even when they are for the better, significant change is always unpleasant in the long run.

Adjusting to new circumstances may be challenging for some of us, especially at first, and it might take some time. As counterintuitive as it may seem, stress may give us the strength to face these challenges.

But stress can also make one feel completely overwhelmed. When stressed, it's hard to keep calm and give it your all as a parent; therefore, the next chapter will examine coping strategies.

# CHAPTER 2: COPING WITH STRESS AND FINDING MEANING IN THE CHAOS

One of the most important things you can do to assist your children in adjusting during this time of change is to set an example of how to handle stress healthily. Having a sense of control over your life might help you feel less stressed and more capable during this time.

This chapter will discuss stress, why your divorce is causing you unwanted stress, why you need to define your responsibilities as a parent, and how you can manage the stressors present in your life.

Once we've worked through the challenging part of this chapter, we'll dedicate some time to reflect on how far you've come, your goals for the future, and how self-reflection builds a strong foundation for positive parenting.

## WHY AM I SO STRESSED?

The body experiences stress as a natural response to change, which manifests in various physical, emotional, and mental reactions. Changes can be harder to deal with when you don't know how to deal with stress.

Everyone will experience the typical human reaction known as stress at some point. The body is made to feel stress and respond to it. When you go through changes or face problems (stressors), your body and mind react differently.

Your body uses stress to help it get used to new situations. Stress can be good for us because it keeps us alert, motivated, and ready to move away from danger. However, stress may become problematic when the factors that cause it persists without being alleviated or replaced with rest times.

## How Much Is Too Much Stress?

Understanding your stress threshold is crucial due to the far-reaching consequences of prolonged or chronic stress. However, the amount of stress that constitutes *too much* for one individual may not be the same for another. While some individuals appear to be able to take all that life throws at them, others tend to buckle under the pressure of even relatively minor setbacks or frustrations.

The following are some of the things that can affect how well you handle stress:

- **Your network of support**: One of the most effective defense mechanisms against the harmful effects of stress is a robust social support system consisting of family and friends. The stresses of daily life aren't so daunting when you have reliable individuals that you can count on. Likewise, the more lonely you are, the more likely you are to get stressed.
- **How in charge you feel**: Maintaining composure in the face of anxiety is much simpler if you have faith in yourself and your capacity to exert some control throughout events and be resilient in the face of adversity. Stress is far more likely to knock you off course if you believe you have little control over your affairs and are primarily at the whim of your surroundings and environment.
- **How you think and feel**: How you think about life and the problems you'll have to face greatly affects how you deal with stress. You will be less likely to get hurt if you are generally upbeat and hopeful. People

who are resilient to stress are more likely to enjoy a challenge, have a better sense of humor, trust in something greater than themselves, and embrace change as an unavoidable aspect of life.

- **How well you can handle your feelings**: It is more probable that you will get tense and irritated if you cannot comfort and reassure yourself when experiencing negative emotions such as sadness, anger, or other difficult emotions. Recognizing and healthily dealing with your emotions can help you handle stress better and bounce back from hard times.
- **How well you know and plan**: Understanding the nature and duration of a stressful event might help you better manage it.

## DID I MAKE THE RIGHT CHOICE?

Having a stable, committed relationship or marriage is becoming increasingly difficult for many individuals. Two individuals choose to marry, but, to their surprise, things frequently change. Circumstances in life, such as time, money, employment, and worry, swoop in and steadily swell beneath the surface, gently tearing two people apart until they divorce one day. When children are involved, the situation becomes considerably more complex and unpleasant. Both parents put an enormous amount of strain on themselves. Chaos, uncertainty, and misunderstanding are expected outcomes that present a bleak image of the *family* dynamic.

Divorce occurs in 40%–50% of all marriages.

There appear to be an infinite number of reasons why individuals decide to break out of a commitment, including disagreements, distrust, stress, money, inequity, power conflicts, violence, adultery, unstated expectations, a lack of passion, and mood swings. The list might go on forever.

Divorced or separated parents experience the following (Isbill, 2020):

- Feelings of regret.
- Shame and guilt.
- Anger and frustration.
- Poor self-esteem and self-worth.
- Depression and a lack of energy.
- Loss of parental control and confidence.
- Critiquing or denouncing the *other parent*.
- Competing for the child's affection and respect.
- The need to please your child instead of leading them.
- Extreme freedom or extreme scrutiny.

Whether married or not, anyone who has gone through a breakup will likely have some unresolved issues from the relationship lingering in their minds. Many people, for example, believe they must constantly prove themselves worthy of other people's affection and esteem. It's possible that both parents and children feel this way subconsciously without even being aware of it until many years later.

Here are some stressors that divorce can cause:

## 1. Negative Thinking Patterns

*Was I the reason you and mommy no longer live together?*

It might seem like an innocent question, but deep down, you have all these worries that become internalized and are never clearly expressed or allowed to be resolved. You struggle to answer the question, keep a smile on your face, and reassure them that it's better this way, while deep down, you're second-guessing the process.

Since you weren't *enough* to keep your previous partner around, it stands to reason that you won't ever be *enough* for your children.

*Why would I ever deserve to be loved again?*

These are harmful and destructive beliefs that easily pierce our emotions, shattering our self-esteem and whatever trace of self-love we may have. Unfortunately, many of us stay oblivious to these inner ideas and sentiments about ourselves until we spend quality alone time, fall into the trustworthy hands of high-quality friends nearby, or consult a respected counselor to help us work through these thoughts. Only after doing so can we see these ideas for what they are: Falsehoods from the outside that we may choose to ignore and reclaim our ability to love ourselves. You have to love yourself before you can love others.

## 2. The Unknown Life of a Single Parent

The proverb "It takes a village to raise a child" is spot on.

Anyone with children can relate to the fact that it's no walk in the park. Parenting is a demanding task in and of itself, but it is considerably more difficult as a single parent. One of the most significant tensions and burdens on each parent's shoulders is the issue of financially providing for their child(ren) on one income.

The sudden loss of one or both parents' wages can devastate a family's financial stability, especially if the new living arrangements require each parent to contribute a considerably larger share of his or her income. Buying a new house in a desirable community as a single mom on a fixed income is practically impossible.

Without shared parental responsibilities and a chance to equalize household wages, single adults face more severe financial hardships than they would as a couple. However, once the marriage separates, the issue of *child support* may be brought up amid high levels of emotion. This is because single parents often experience feelings of dread and scarcity. After all, they have significantly less money available to provide for themselves and their children after paying for necessities such as food and housing.

Given how busy and cramped our lives have become, it's no surprise that we're all frantically seeking solace from others who, like us, struggle to find it in their own lives.

When a relationship between two parents ends, the two parents themselves suffer, as do any children they may have together. Friends, family, children, instructors, and employees must all learn to engage with single people rather than couples.

### 3. No More Reminiscing About Old Times

Most people's friends and family rarely discuss their relationships with one another because they are terrified of saying the *wrong* thing. Having a healthy family can often result in the parents losing their previously held friendships and family members and the support they provide. More important resources are squandered, and the strains on single parents' shoulders continue to mount.

Since marriage is predicated on the idea that two people join together to form a single entity, it follows that when the newly formed *one* decides to separate back into *two*, both partners suffer significant losses on all levels of being. Of course, this is a difficult period. It may also be a highly confusing situation for the children. If things get out of hand, consult a therapist who focuses on helping families through breakups and reunification.

*How do you even start talking about your divorce with your children? I don't know where to begin. All I want for them is happiness. I don't want to upset them.*

These are frequent thoughts expressed by parents who have gone through this process. An enlightening podcast that tackles complex topics head-on is one of the numerous resources you have available to connect your children to this necessary but challenging talk.

Counseling opportunities are another key option to explore. This might be the ideal moment to focus on your mental health. You might also try attending with your previous partner. Although it may appear strange, families tend to collaborate for the good of their children. A mediator can act as a barrier between you and your ex, allowing you to sort out your differences and go forward as separate parents. The decision to seek professional help, as some parents do with family and family therapy, may provide valuable information and a secure environment where all parties can be emotionally present and open with one another. You don't have to go through this alone.

*What are your responsibilities during this time?*

## Defining My Role as a Parent

There are instances when grownups have trouble knowing what they are *meant* to do for their child since the lines have blurred. You do not need to be flawless, but you must be present.

What's your role as a parent?

- Take charge in a just manner, considering your child's best interests.
- Assist them in making good choices for themselves.

- Give them the knowledge they need to survive in this chaotic world.
- Lean in with compassion and set a good example.

What role do you *not* play as a parent?

- **Always wanting to be correct**: If you say that your way of raising the child is better than the other parent's, it breaks the child's connection with the other parent and makes it harder for the child to understand both parents.
- **Micro-managing your child's life**: To scrutinize every aspect of your child's life to ascertain the other parent's influence on your child.
- **Suppress your or your child's emotions**: As you openly and honestly discuss your experiences and emotions with your child, help them interact with their own.
- **Win over your child with gifts**: Your child's love and affection should not be bought to show the other parent that you're the *better* parent. All your child asks for is quality time spent with each parent.

Similarly, your anguish is their anguish. Your approach to overcoming these obstacles will serve as a model for your child. You can't keep them safe in a damaged world full of broken people; they will be more likely to face difficulties with the same happiness, optimism, and positivity if they see you face them the same way. Don't avoid challenging situations; be optimistic and lead the way.

## Words Are Louder Than Action

I want you to consider the words you use—both spoken and unsaid. You may not be aware of it, but your behavior already reflects your innermost thoughts and feelings about yourself and the other parent. It's crucial to give your feelings toward the other adult and the way the connection developed some serious thought. Both adults must know how they feel about their parenting abilities and those of others. Your inner monologue will seep out into your speech, then your behavior, and finally into your parenting.

How to be more mindful, observant, and kind:

- Keep an eye on what you say beneath your breath. They might be either positive or negative, beneficial, or harmful.
- Take note of your reactions in the mirror as you recall specific events and people from your previous relationship.
- Have early and frequent conversations with your child about your bond. Your avoidance may leave them with an emptiness that they may only hope to fill through uncertainty and misunderstanding.
- Make an effort to keep the other parent in the loop on your child's major life events, such as his or her first visit to the dentist, a meeting with the child's teacher, the onset of puberty, and yes, even when it's time for *the talk*. Before diving in headfirst or reacting impulsively without a chance to consider your words, it's wise to have an objective.

- Support. You, your child, and the other parent. Nobody wants to be wounded, and everyone intends to give it their all.

**You Can Do This**

Even if your previous relationship ended badly, you and your ex-partner might still work together as co-parents to help your child develop socially and emotionally. While it may be challenging, try your best.

Who knows what you could inspire in the other parent or what kind of supportive partnership you could build for the sake of your beloved children?

If everything else fails, if the other parent refuses to collaborate with you or is absent, accept that you can only affect the events directly within your sphere of influence. You have complete control over your life's ideals and connection with your child. You have complete control over creating a nurturing, caring environment for your child to develop in and enjoy throughout their lives.

The other parent in your child's life is beyond your control, but you can have an impact by using your parental authority and leadership. You may love and nurture as much as you want.

Allow your child or children to open up to you, and then listen to them, guiding and supporting them as they do so.

Make an effort to be present.

Your presence is, without a doubt, the most valuable present that you could give.

## PRACTICAL WAYS TO MANAGE THE STRESSES OF DIVORCE

No matter what led to the breakup of the marriage, going through the divorce or separation process may be extremely challenging. Your day-to-day routine may be thrown off, and you may find it difficult to get anything done. There are things you can do to help you get through this challenging transition.

Here are some practical strategies for managing stress during or after your divorce:

- **Recognize that it is perfectly normal to have a variety of emotions**: It is natural to experience negative emotions such as sadness, anger, exhaustion, frustration, and confusion, and the intensity of these sensations should not be surprising. You may also be experiencing feelings of anxiety about the future. Recognize that with time, responses like this will become less frequent. Leaving the familiar, even if it is harmful, may be terrifying.
- **Take a step back and breathe**: You should give yourself the go-ahead to feel and perform at a less-than-ideal level for a certain amount of time. Your normal levels of productivity at work and compassion for others may temporarily diminish. Take the time to mend, gather, and regain your strength; no one is a superhero.
- **Don't go through all of this alone**: It might be helpful to talk about how you're feeling with people you know and care about, such as friends and family. Think about joining a support group so you can share

your experiences with others going through something similar. Isolating yourself may cause you to feel more stressed, make it harder for you to concentrate, and make it more difficult to focus on your career, relationships, and general health. If you need assistance from a third party, do not hesitate to ask for it.

- **Take care of your mental and physical health**: Take care of both your mind and your physical being. Make it a priority to exercise, maintain a healthy diet, and unwind. Maintain as much consistency as you can with your typical practices. Make it a point to steer clear of making significant life changes or choices. As a coping mechanism, avoid using drugs, alcohol, or tobacco, as these simply worsen the situation.
- **Spend some time exploring the things that interest you**: Get back in touch with activities you love doing on your own, apart from your partner. Have you always been interested in picking up a paintbrush or joining a softball team at your local university? Enroll in a course, devote some of your time to activities you like, lend a helping hand to others, and don't forget to take some time to relax, have fun, and meet new acquaintances.
- **Think about the bright side**: It's easier to say than accomplish, right? This shift will be less difficult if you engage in new pursuits and develop new connections with others, as well as if you have your sights set on the future and set realistic goals for yourself. Be adaptable.

There will come a time when life returns to *normal,* even if this *normal* may not be what you initially envisioned for yourself.

## A TIME FOR SELF-REFLECTION

Beginning the process of reinventing yourself as soon as possible is the most effective method to reduce the stress of going through a divorce. Find strategies to give yourself time to grieve and process your emotions as soon as you can after losing a loved one. A therapist could be of some assistance. At the very least, you should surround yourself with upbeat individuals who can show you how to find the silver lining in every situation.

You must learn to appreciate who you are to recover who you used to be or recreate who you are. This is the first and most critical step. After getting divorced, you can go through a period in which you reject yourself excessively. You may work on regaining your confidence by challenging yourself to accomplish a few simple tasks, such as getting out of bed after a lengthy period of staying in bed and going to the mailbox. After that, you may go on to getting ready, going out, and doing something nice to feel better about yourself again.

Find yourself responsible for paying the bills or taking on a new sort of obligation that your partner previously handled. You should feel proud of your new role. Your tension will gradually decrease if you are willing to accept the changes that are occurring.

Consider the benefits of spending time alone occasionally. You are free to act according to your desires and those of your children and are not required to take anybody else's advice. If that's what you want, a temporary connection could help keep your mind off things. This is not to be looked at as a rebound; rather, it is more analogous to testing the waters of the dating world after a divorce by going on a few dates.

Suppose you can maintain a positive attitude throughout the divorce process. In that case, you will find that the tension associated with the situation will quickly fade away.

## The Aftermath of Divorce: Considerations

You may improve your chances of happiness in future relationships by applying the knowledge you gained from your previous marriage.

The majority of individuals view divorce as evidence of a failed relationship. Divorce may be a failure, but just like any other failure, there are lessons to be learned from it. The issue is that many of us either do not know how to seek such lessons or do not want to look for them.

The lessons you learn by thinking back on your marriage's ups and downs, even if difficult, may be invaluable. You will get a deeper understanding of who you are, what you desire, what you require, and what you can provide to another person.

Start by asking yourself these eight questions if you are unsure how to get started:

### 1. Who Am I? What Do I Want?

When you were younger, you probably envisioned yourself working as a veterinarian. Still, now that you're an adult, you're in sales. Perhaps all through high school, you dreamed of relocating to the West Coast, yet here you are, a few decades later, still residing in the Big Apple. Things evolve as a result of life. Life transforms us.

You and your partner may have different priorities today than before you were married. Even the goals you had when you were married could be different from the ones you have now that you are no longer married. Before and throughout your marriage, you were different from who you are today.

To get the most out of life, you need to spend quality time thinking about yourself, your goals, and your aspirations. There's always the chance that once you think you're done having children, you'll change your mind and desire more. Once you have a firm grasp on your identity and what you seek from life, you can devise a strategy to achieve your goals.

### 2. How Would I Describe My Former Partner if They Weren't My Ex?

It's easy to forget that your ex had any redeeming traits among all the bitterness and pain you've been feeling over your breakup and the events leading up to it.

When co-parenting, however, we can't afford to accept the nihilistic view that our ex-partner is complete without redeeming traits. Consider for a moment if your last romantic partner was someone entirely different. What are your thoughts on them in general? What kind of a description would you give them? What would you tell someone who knew them as a friend, a coworker, or a casual acquaintance?

### 3. If My Ex Were Someone Else, What Would They Say About Me?

Suppose you continue to think and speak negatively about your ex-partner. In that case, you can be assured that they also think and speak negatively about you. However, in the same way, that it may help you cope with your ex better if you remind yourself of their positive traits, it can also be helpful to remember that they may still have some positive things to say about you.

It may also put what you've done or are doing in perspective. It can assist you in identifying areas where you are being blinded by your own emotions and recognizing where you could be saying or even doing things you would not say or do if you were not experiencing so much anger and hurt.

Think about what your ex may tell a friend, coworker, or neighbor if they heard negative things about you from them. Do you think it would make you happy?

### 4. Am I Giving This Relationship the Best Version of Myself?

Significant factors might contribute to the decision to end your marriage, such as one partner's unfaithfulness or addiction. And the reason may lie with your former partner. But in many cases, if you give yourself some time to reflect on the past genuinely, you may discover that there are things that you might have done better that would have resulted in a happier marriage.

Don't get the wrong idea; I'm not suggesting that you're to blame if your partner cheats on you or develops an addiction to substances like alcohol or drugs. However, you may see that you were preoccupied with your job and children to the point that your partner felt neglected and, rather than coming to you to try to work things out, went out and had an affair.

Asking yourself this question may be useful because it can help you reflect on what went wrong in the relationship and provide insight into how you might improve the way you act in future partnerships.

### 5. **Did I Coast While My Partner Worked?**

Work is required in relationships, and neither partner can accomplish it alone. However, one partner may shoulder the responsibility in an unhealthy, imbalanced relationship. At the same time, the other does little more than hang out. Examining yourself to determine whether or not you may have contributed to the marriage breakup is essential, even if you believe that most of the fault lies with your former partner.

You shouldn't only search for laziness in the larger picture, either. Think about the little responsibilities you may have delegated to your partner, such as taking care of the children, managing the money, or communicating with extended relatives. Something that seemed small at the time—or even something that your partner appreciated—might have contributed to the final dissolution of your marriage.

If you find items like that, you should investigate why they occurred. Perhaps you find it stressful to deal with the bills, so you delegate much of the responsibility to your partner. It's important to discuss this with your next potential partner early on so that you can work together to find a solution that works for both of you.

### 6. Did My Partner Work Less Because I Did So Much?

When one partner does everything while the other gets off easy, resentment generally results. There are several possible explanations for why you might have done anything like this. You may have picked a partner who was unmotivated and unwilling to help. It's possible that you wanted to feel like you were in charge of the relationship. It's possible that you witnessed this in the relationship between your parents.

If you have been carrying most of the burden, you must acknowledge this and examine the reasons behind your behavior. After you have accomplished that, the next stage is to determine how to prevent yourself from making that mistake. What steps do you need to take so your partner can take responsibility for their portion of the relationship?

Be willing to search deeply to obtain these answers. If you did it in one relationship, then it is quite probable that you have done it in previous relationships. Finding out the answer to this question can make a significant difference in the subsequent connection you have.

### 7. What Are Some of the Biggest Mistakes I've Made?

There are certain people for whom this is the question with the simplest response. For some people, this is the one inquiry they would give anything to be able to steer clear of for good. However, it is also a connection that may teach you invaluable lessons about yourself and the kind of person you should seek out in the future.

What would you change about marriage and divorce if you could go back in time? What would you change about the way you handled the situation? In what ways do you wish things had gone differently with your partner? Is there anything you wish had been different?

### 8. What Would I Have Done Differently to Maintain My Marriage and Sanity if I Hadn't Decided to Divorce?

We're lucky to live in a society where divorce is legally possible for most people. Some people may protest that it's too simple. What if, though, that wasn't the case? What if you were forced to remain married to your former partner and didn't have the choice to get a divorce?

If you could do it again, what would you change about your marriage to your ex that would have kept you from going completely crazy? What aspects of your relationship might you have worked on to improve it, establish common ground, or make your marriage more fulfilling and joyful?

It is not always easy to find the answers to these questions, particularly in cases where there was physical or emotional abuse or adultery that played a role in the dissolution of the marriage. However, this is also highly beneficial since you may find places where you realize you have worked a little more. Looking at this can be helpful. And having that awareness can aid you in the relationships you have in the future. Once you have this knowledge, you'll be able to identify your areas for improvement and make progress in those areas.

See your divorce as a fresh start.

A divorce may feel like the end of something, but it is the start of something new. It's a new beginning and an opportunity to reassess how you've been handling love and relationships up until now. No matter how quickly or slowly you end a marriage, there is at least one item you can take away from the experience that will help you have more success in subsequent romantic partnerships.

And it's alright if you're still processing the breakup and aren't ready to start posing these questions to yourself. You should allow yourself some time to recover from this. But if you wait too long, you risk seeing the past in a different light than it was.

## POSITIVE PARENTING AND SELF-REFLECTION

The work of raising a child (or children) is challenging and gratifying; it requires a lot of time and energy, offers few opportunities for rest or relaxation, and comes with no instructions. Even though there are plenty of tools to assist parents in improving their parenting skills, occasionally, we've put ourselves in emotionally taxing circumstances that don't allow us to be the most effective parents we can all be.

Our words around our children form their internal dialogue, and our responses to various life events serve as models for them to follow. To put it another way, our children benefit most when we're at our best. If we want to be the best children of ourselves, we need to take a step back and examine our inner workings sometimes.

Self-reflection that helps parents improve their communication and connections with their children entails tuning in to and processing their feelings. Self-reflection on being a good parent should also include considering the goals and ideals we have towards ourselves, our connections with our children, and how we raise them.

## The First Steps Toward a More Reflective Approach to Parenting

Having a positive influence on your child's development is possible. Still, it requires time, energy, and dedication to master an authoritative parenting style. Self-reflection helps us maintain our resolve (and our sanity) in the face of adversity since the rewards don't come immediately.

It might be challenging to incorporate self-reflection into your daily routine since many of us are not trained. If you want to start using constructive self-reflection as a parent, consider the following:

1. **Start a Journal**

Take 5–10 minutes out of your day to jot down your ideas and emotions, either on paper or in the notes app on your phone. Use journaling prompts or free-write on how you feel about your child's circumstances or behavior.

Let's assume you and your child have been having difficulty getting to sleep for a long time, and your irritation levels are through the roof. Sit back and think about the events leading up to bedtime now that your little one is asleep. How would you rate my afternoon disposition? What will happen if I talk in a quiet tone? When I become angry, what happens? In what ways is my child picking up on the feelings I'm expressing?

### 2. **Focus on the Present Moment**

It's easy to gloss over emotions amid the day's activities. By the time we get home, we're too spent to think about them.

Most of the time, it is challenging to take a vacation from a challenging parenting scenario. Stopping a 10 a.m. grocery store meltdown to jot down our emotions is unrealistic. However, we may always take some time soon after that to dwell back on such experiences in detail.

Spend a minute or two after a tough parenting moment writing down your feelings and thoughts. Take a moment to consider your emotions as they arise. You'll have a better chance of recalling every nuance of your experience and making it simpler to address underlying issues.

If you need to go there but don't have time to stop and think, try recording your ideas on the voice memo feature on your phone.

### 3. Find Some Time for Yourself

We all know how difficult it is to find some quiet time for ourselves. Although taking a break now and then is important, having *time alone* doesn't require complete isolation; it only necessitates some time to reflect.

Use the time while your child is in the contact-napping or stroller-walking period to be engaged with your feelings and thoughts; this means no podcasts, radio, or social networking sites.

In this day of continual connectivity, it may be easy to lose touch with our emotions and forget how it feels to be alone with our thoughts. Remember to prioritize your requirements before worrying about anybody else's when you take a break from providing for others.

Incorporate reflective practices like stretching and mental imagery into your warm-up and pre-workout routines if you have time to yourself as part of your routine, such as when you exercise. Rather than struggling to create more time alone, put the time you currently have to good use.

## Valuable Questions to Ask Oneself While Reflecting

Many mature individuals find that it is useful to use prompts during times of self-reflection. Here is a selection of questions to consider during your quiet time of introspection.

Do not let the difficulty of this exercise make you feel horrible about yourself; instead, use it as a chance to tune into your own needs and desires as a parent.

Questions for general introspection:

- How can I instill in my children the morals and principles I hope they'll carry into adulthood?
- Which approach to parenting do I feel most at ease with?
- Do I prioritize my own needs and well-being?
- Is my ability to parent impacted by any particular sources of stress?
- To what extent do my co-parent and I strive toward our shared parenting goals?
- For me, as a parent, what resources would be most reliable?

### Improve Your Parenting Through Introspection

The following questions guide you in establishing the best possible version of yourself for your children.

The questions are as follows:

- Which of the top five fundamental values do I believe is my responsibility as a parent to teach my children?
- In what ways do I want my children to grow and mature this year?
- Do I tend to parent more from an emotional response or from constant rational consequences and communication?
- What do my children consider most important in their lives?
- How am I doing in terms of developing meaningful relationships with my children?
- How effective are my co-parenting efforts with my current partner?

- Do I give myself enough time to relax and recharge? Am I making space for my child to engage in peaceful play?
- How true to myself am I when I talk to my children? By being upfront and honest with them, am I laying the foundation for future trust and safety?
- Do my children presently give or take more often? Do they actively seek opportunities to help others even when I'm not pushing them to?
- How grateful am I for my loved ones? Do my children currently show thankfulness regularly?

This chapter discussed why you're feeling the way you do and what you can do to relieve stress. The following will look at all the nitty-gritty things associated with co-parenting.

# CHAPTER 3: CO-PARENTING AND MY CHILD

Divorce or separation brings its own emotions and obstacles to parenting, making it feel like it's nearly impossible to do effectively at times.

This book was created because I recognize the difficulties associated with co-parenting and want to help you overcome them.

This book might not solve all your problems as a co-parent, but it will help make things easier and more satisfying for everyone involved. The resources I've gathered in this chapter will help you and your co-parenting partner establish and sustain a positive dynamic in your family.

This chapter will briefly overview co-parenting principles, how your child might experience the new shift in the family dynamic, how they can benefit from the separation, and what it will teach them about life.

## CO-PARENTING PRINCIPLES

It's challenging to learn how to co-parent. There are many underlying issues and wrongs from the past that might sour your relationship with your co-parent. However, for your child to thrive, a team effort is required. Here are some helpful guidelines from licensed Newport Divorce attorneys if you have co-parenting difficulties.

### What Is Co-Parenting?

When a child's two parents decide to divide custody of their children, this is referred to as "co-parenting." This may occur if a couple divorces' or separates. Many couples choose to co-parent, but it is a challenging decision to make. It gives their children a chance to interact with both parents. It enables them to take part in significant life milestones. However, co-parenting is not always simple, and resentment or irritation can rapidly rise to the point of erupting. Thankfully, many parents have successfully applied their beneficial co-parenting concepts, allowing you to succeed.

*Here are some positive guidelines for successful co-parenting:*

Communication, consistency, and mutual support are the essential characteristics that have proven useful for co-parents. You and your ex-partner may give your children the best possible life by adhering to these constructive co-parenting practices.

## Communication

Although it may sound cliche, communication is crucial. You must communicate your expectations to your ex-partner if you and your partner have any going into the co-parenting arrangement. An open communication channel, well-defined limits, and a readiness to hear one another are necessary. Although you could have different parenting philosophies and engagement levels, there should be respect between you that transcends your prior issues.

One of the essential elements of communication is compromised. Considerable difficulties are usually settled amicably if both parties treat each other with dignity and listen to the other side of the argument. Knowing that you and your ex-partner may have open communication about any issue makes it much simpler to voice your concerns and find common ground.

## Consistency

An essential part of co-parenting is maintaining consistency and open lines of communication. Before you begin co-parenting, you and your ex-partner will need to settle on ground rules, a system of discipline, and a routine that works for everyone involved. Who will pick up the children from school, transport them to their after-school activities, etc.? Will all of this be accounted for in a timetable? Maintaining a routine aids in your child's adjustment to this new way of life. While maintaining a regular schedule is something you should aim for, unexpected events may happen, so you should be adaptable. You need to be able to communicate whether your job requires you to put in more hours if you wish to go with your child on vacation or even if you simply desire to take them to a soccer game one day.

Additionally, you must be adaptable enough to accept these modifications if your ex-partner wants them.

Similarly, before co-parenting, it is crucial to clarify the rules and the appropriate sanctions for breaching them. If your child can kick the ball around the house in one household, they may wonder why they're being reprimanded in another. Your child may get anxious and overwhelmed by the recent changes in his or her life due to this uncertainty. No matter whose home they are in, it is crucial to uphold the same standards and the proper disciplinary techniques.

### Cooperation

The two of you are now functioning as one. If you want to succeed as a team in parenting your child, you have to be able to put aside your differences with your colleagues, even if you don't like them. You should thus be your ex's ally. A partner's Placing your child amid disagreements or conflicts is unjust to them. It is unacceptable to use your child as leverage against their other parent, regardless of how supportive or joyful you are.

Keeping your child away from confrontation is another crucial consideration. You can disagree with one another and dispute in a setting where your child won't witness it. Any remaining tension, however, must be resolved, and a unified front must be presented to the child. Similarly, you should be considerate of one another's time spent with the children. You cannot ruin someone else's time by interfering if one parent has them over the weekend. Take advantage of your time with your child while allowing your ex-partner to enjoy theirs.

## MY CHILD AND COPING WITH CHANGE

Many things affect how well children can handle a divorce. Some of these factors can be changed by what we do, while others may be out of our hands. Families may need as many as five years to fully recover from the effects of a divorce, according to studies, depending on the specifics of the situation (McGhee, 2013).

Parents need to know that their children will react in different ways. Some of them may be short-term responses to the fact that divorce is a crisis. Others have long-term effects that could be good or bad, depending on how well parents can help their children.

### Will My Child Adjust to the Divorce?

Are you concerned about how your child will adjust to the new family dynamic?

McGhee (2013) lists some things that can affect how well someone adjusts:

### How Much Trouble There Is Between Parents

The level of disagreement is one of the most influential aspects of children's adjustment. It can be very bad for children if their parents always fight, criticize the other parent, or fight over custody. When parents can put aside their differences and work together, it dramatically affects how well their children adjust. Don't let what the other parent does change your feelings about your child. You may still be a steady, positive influence on your children even if you and your ex-partner don't get along if you consciously decide to avoid fights and keep things "businesslike."

### How Parents Get Used to Being Separated

The degree to which parents can accept and move on from the divorce is a significant determinant of how well the child agrees with the split. Children will look to you for reassurance that your family will be okay. Parents must provide a good example of the complexity of the emotions involved in a divorce. Parents can also help their children feel like they are part of a family by being consistent and setting rules. Your decisions can and will have lasting consequences for your children. Your children will do much better if they make good decisions.

### When They're Told About the Divorce

Keep the following things in mind to ensure your children get information that is good for them:

- Make sure your children know your affection for them and that they are not to blame for your divorce.
- Keep the information appropriate for their age.
- Address the children's immediate worries, such as where they will reside and whether they will attend the same school.
- Keep fights with the other parent to a minimum. Avoid verbal retaliation.

- Don't talk to children about grown-up things like court cases, child support, money, or intimate details about the divorce.
- Do not tell your children that their other parent is at fault or that you are right, and have them believe you.

## The Child's Age and Level of Development

When it comes to divorce, many parents are curious as to what age their children will be least affected. There is no optimal age for a marriage to end in divorce. Different problems and challenges come up at different ages and stages of development. Parents should know what normal child development looks like and pay attention to changes in their child's behavior.

## The Level of Support

For the sake of your children, it is best to keep as much of their routine as possible after a divorce or separation. Because divorce can make a child feel anxious or afraid, keeping up with school, outside activities, or friends in the neighborhood can help. Maintaining relationships with prominent relatives on both sides of the family should also be a priority. Children need to feel like they can talk to someone safely about their feelings. It doesn't have to be a trained professional; it might be someone like a friend, family member, clergy member, teacher, or school counselor. Check with local schools and religious groups to see if they have programs to help children and families going through a divorce.

### The Behavior of Your Child

Children will react differently to different situations and events. Even children from the same family will react differently to divorce. Some children can handle pressure better than others, while others might act out or shut down when things get tough. Pay close attention, above all else, to the hints your child is providing you with through how they behave. If their behavior changes a lot or stays the same for six months or more, you should talk to a professional.

### The Capacity of Your Child to Handle Pressure

Children have different personalities and deal with stress differently. Not all children will react similarly to the stress of a parent's separation or divorce. You will be doing your child a considerable service if you can assist them in locating healthy coping mechanisms for both the emotions they are experiencing and the pressures they are under. Additionally, ensure that you and your children have plenty of opportunities to talk to one another.

## WILL MY CHILDREN BENEFIT FROM THE DIVORCE?

Here is a quick guide on how your children can benefit from divorce.

The following may happen to children of divorced parents:

- A calmer atmosphere at home.
- Better communication between each child and each parent.

- A sense of anticipation about getting to celebrate holidays and birthdays twice, with assistance from other single-parent children.
- A greater understanding of how to establish and respect personal boundaries.

Let's take an in-depth look at why having a divorce might be a good thing for your children:

1. **Better Parental Well-Being**

Your family's dynamic will undoubtedly alter after divorce. This might bring renewed happiness to you and your ex-partner. The tensions between you have subsided or disappeared entirely. You can start your new life as a single parent with a calm assurance you never felt in marriage.

Even if it takes some time, your children will likely experience this change in your mental health. Since children can sense parental tension, they will also notice when you can let part of it go.

Children of divorce with one parent functioning well tend to perform better than those without parents (Williams, 2021).

It goes without saying that your emotions won't improve immediately. It's possible that single parenting has new negative impacts on you, and it's easy to get so preoccupied with home management details that you lose touch with your emotions.

Your children will react to your divorce somewhat similarly to how you did (even if their perspective is different). By taking care of yourself, you can change how the impacts of divorce manifest for you. Happy parents result in happy children!

2. **Stronger Bonds With Each Parent**

If you and your partner are having problems, you may find it challenging to focus on maintaining a close bond with your children. You may have less time to spend with them while the divorce is finalized.

But you could feel calmer if you're a parent whose spouse has formally divorced. After the divorce, you could have more energy to invest in your connection with your children. Your ex-partner may be able to say the same.

Your children will spend time with you on their own, giving you a great chance to create or strengthen emotional safety, a foundational element of good child development and positive adult relationships.

3. **Provide Twice as Much Support and Fun Occasions**

Divorce's positive effects on children include a co-parenting arrangement that allows them to participate in two sets of significant life events simultaneously.

Many individuals segregate birthday celebrations from holiday customs when transitioning from two-parent to single-parent homes. This implies that your children may get twice as many Thanksgiving meals, cakes, and presents as they are used to. Most of them, particularly the younger children, are okay with this result of divorce!

When parents split their time between them, a child can experience more than just good times. Having the opportunity to connect with relatives on both sides of the family in new or different ways might provide emotional assistance.

You could need childcare assistance from your family if

you're a single parent, whether you're a custodial parent or not. It also means that your children will get used to their cousins, grandparents, and other members of the extended family.

### 4. New Relationships With Families With Single Parents

Having a support system may help alleviate the effects of divorce. If they're purposeful about forging new relationships, divorce allows children to mingle with others whose family structures are comparable to their own.

Look for other divorced parents to give your child a feeling of community (Williams, 2021):

- If you just relocated, go to neighborhood events.
- At your child's activities, introduce yourself to the parents.
- Look for local or online gatherings for single parents.
- Get to know the other members by enrolling in a class or joining a gym.
- Your acquaintances' children may eventually become close family friends with yours.

Even if your children are too young or unwilling to discuss divorce directly with their new friends, they will see how their peers similarly move back and forth between homes. They'll feel less embarrassed about accepting their situation.

Children might feel less alone and divorced, and mixed families can become more normal thanks to the social support of other divorced families. According to the American Psychological Association, a child's ability to cope with adversity may be considerably increased by having a strong social support system (Williams, 2021).

### 5. The Knowledge of Healthy Boundaries

There are several chances to provide children with appropriate limits due to all the changes that divorce might bring. They may have the opportunity to gain crucial social skills that children of married parents may not have.

If you want your children to see the divorce as a positive experience rather than a blow to their self-esteem, mastering boundary-setting is crucial.

With your post-divorce encounters, you'll have plenty of opportunities to practice:

- **Your children could see you and the other parent establishing boundaries**: They'll learn that parental dispute (and therefore other sorts of relationship conflict they see) doesn't always have to end in catastrophe if they observe both of you establishing limits respectfully. You might even tell your child that you're communicating with your ex-partner to discuss shared spending, showing them how well-functioning post-divorce collaboration can be.
- **You may sometimes need to explain to a caregiver what is allowed or necessary under your co-parenting agreement**: For instance, you may need to let the gymnastics coach of your daughter know that her father has to be included in all team communications. If it is acceptable, let your child hear

these talks so they may learn that other people can adjust to this shift in their lives.

- **Remarrying or moving in with a significant other again may be out of the question right now. Still, it's never too early to start thinking about the future:** Plan to set boundaries with your former partner, new partner, and children. Let your children witness you standing up for them when the time comes.

All ages benefit from witnessing adults establish good boundaries. Still, teenagers in high school need one since they are about to start dating seriously. In a later chapter, we'll look at how you can help your children set healthy boundaries.

Keep an open mind on the positive impact divorce may have on the children.

Most children don't see or want to experience parental separation when they think about their future. Love plays the most significant role in a child's existence. Two single-parent homes may provide as much love and support as whole families.

Divorce may benefit children if you see it as an opportunity to learn vital lessons and experience greater love. We'll take a closer look at how a divorce might benefit your child. The following section will examine how your child is affected by divorce and how you can support them.

# SECTION 2: UNDERSTANDING YOUR CHILD'S EMOTIONAL DEVELOPMENT

Divorce is sometimes the only option for many individuals. Undoubtedly, this is a very stressful period for everyone involved. When parents separate, this is true for the children involved, especially the younger ones, who may not completely comprehend the reasons for the breakdown of their family structure. It may be difficult for children when their parents divorce; many children deal with it differently and may start acting differently due to this traumatic experience. Remember how it affects your child when going through a divorce, and do all you can to help them cope.

This section explores how your child might be affected during this time—know what to expect for each age group for the first year after divorce. Understand how you can support them and what they need to succeed.

# CHAPTER 4: HOW IS MY CHILD AFFECTED?

One of the most important things you can do is help your child adjust to the *new normal.*

This chapter will discuss the effects of divorce on your child, the behaviors you can expect, and how you can work through the more challenging parts together.

## THE NEW NORMAL

Your relationships as a couple and as parents are intertwined when you and the other parent are raising your children together. After a divorce or separation, developing a new connection with the other parent is necessary for co-parenting your child or children.

The primary focus of partnerships based on co-parenting is doing what is in the best interests of the child or children involved. There are numerous different configurations for couples who are co-parenting. Many things, including your compatibility with the other parent, will determine the type of your co-parenting relationship. For instance, some parents can talk about their children in person with one another. Others find this challenging, so they opt to contact one another by email or text message, and only when it's essential.

If your connection with your child's other parent is strained, adhere to these rules:

1. You can only hold each other to the terms spoken or explicitly agreed upon in writing.
2. Maintain formality in your interactions with the other parent by ensuring that your get-togethers occur at predetermined times and in neutral settings (like a coffee shop) and that you both come prepared with a list of topics to be covered.
3. Stay away from being too emotionally invested in one another.
4. If it is not directly relevant to parenting, you should avoid exchanging personal information with one another.
5. Do not place undue weight on what is written in emails and messages. The person whose messages or emails come across as angry or sarcastic did not intend for them to be interpreted in that manner at all.
6. Find a method of communication suitable for the two of you, and then pick a realistic turnaround time for responses.

It will take time for the dynamic between the parents to shift from that of a pair to that of co-parents. You are going to have to put in a lot of effort. It may take some time before the other parent, and you figure out how to interact effectively as co-parents.

## TRAUMATIC LOSS

It may be painful when a parent and their children go through a divorce. Still, they don't always get the help they need or even recognize the severity of the situation. There are typical emotions of loss, sadness, wrath, betrayal, remorse, and humiliation following a breakup, regardless of the reasons behind it. Both parents may be saddened once a marriage breaks down. The stress may cause them to experience primal and potent feelings of abandonment, loneliness, and dread. Depression or anxiety may result from this. When you are vulnerable and emotionally fragile, it is difficult to provide your children with the necessary things. When you are vulnerable and emotionally fragile, it is difficult to provide your children with the necessary things. When a marriage fails, things might get more difficult for you and your children, both practically and logistically. Divorce frequently causes financial hardship and social problems. Children may think that they are to blame for their parent's separation. They may feel unworthy, nervous, and sad due to guilt and shame. Suppose the parents cannot communicate with each other. In that case, every aspect of their lives—including living arrangements, extracurricular activities, educational decisions, and holidays—can be riddled with tension.

When you start the divorce and separation process, you may feel a lack of liking or trust for your partner. Being separated from the children while they are in the care of their other parent —possibly your least favorite person under the circumstances—

can be incredibly painful and unpleasant. Real worries regarding the safety of the children in your ex's custody may exist, sometimes in connection with drug or alcohol usage. When one parent has custody of their children, some parents worry that their children may be subjected to abuse by the other parent. However, in two families, the children must generally locate a safe space for themselves. They must be supported in feeling at home in both settings. The serenity and lack of conflict for the children following a divorce might occasionally be a comfort.

### Parents in Conflict

A child must learn to distinguish between the *good* and the *bad* when both parents are on opposite sides of the conflict. A child may feel insecure and mistrustful of his father if his mother believes, for example, that the mother's ex-husband is dangerous or cruel. The child may turn against the father to protect themselves and their mother from potential psychological damage. A child may find it challenging to trust and love a parent that the other despises.

Try to avoid engaging in a win-or-lose conflict with an ex unless it is unavoidable due to your circumstances. In this war, children are virtually always the victims.

When their parents cannot end their marriage courteously, civilly, and peacefully, they may feel torn apart. It is essential to protect the cherished mental image that the child has of themselves with both their biological parents because this representation will serve as the foundation of your child's identity when they grow up.

A key piece of advice for parents who have experienced a divorce is to work as hard as possible to maintain their connection with their ex-partner—who will forever be the children's other parent, for better or worse. Try to co-parent respectfully, constructively, and cooperatively for the benefit of your children.

## The Effects of Divorce on Children

Even when parents' divorce peacefully, it may still be difficult and unpleasant for the child. They could have trouble controlling their emotions, which could cause them to act out, withdraw, have attachment problems, or engage in dangerous activities. Even though the repercussions of divorce can often continue for years, the first year after a divorce is frequently the most difficult for children. However, children frequently learn to cope with this battle and the accompanying unpleasant emotions.

Parents may assist their children in adjusting to this shift in life and lessen the probability of negative effects by providing them with plenty of support, care, and attention.

As parents, we must fine-tune our ability to learn about and listen to our children's hidden emotions. The following is a list of what they might experience or try to hide during this trying time.

Divorce may have several unintended consequences, such as:

### 1. Anger

Anger is a frequent emotion that children feel both during and after their parents' divorce. If the divorce is high-conflict, children may have trouble controlling their emotions owing to physiological stress. This leads to rage and physical aggression, even if these behaviors are employed to cover other feelings that are more fundamentally driving the situation. Children frequently express their resentment against the parent who requested the divorce or whom they believe to be to blame for the divorce. However, their rage might be more general than aimed at a specific individual.

2. **Withdrawal**

Children who experience their parents' divorce may become socially reclusive or steer clear of past interests or pastimes. These habits are more prevalent in divorces with a lot of disputes. There are several potential causes for this. Children may, for instance, feel responsible or guilty for their parent's divorce, which causes them to internalize and isolate their symptoms. Children may experience guilt about their parent's divorce, which makes them avoid situations where they can be questioned about their family in public.

3. **Absence of School Interest**

Children who have experienced divorce are more likely than their non-divorced peers to have poorer attendance, less homework, lower grades, greater rates of school dropout, and less parental supervision of academics at home.

This might be because they are preoccupied with negative feelings or have to take on extra domestic duties after the divorce. However, the results are noticeably better when dads are actively involved in their children's education and complete their schoolwork.

### 4. Attachment and Relationship Problems

Divorce frequently has an adverse effect on children's ability to form healthy, stable relationships because it might make parental resources unpredictable or unavailable.

High-intensity parental arguing is linked to more anxious and insecure bonding in newborns and toddlers. Furthermore, research indicates that childhood attachment problems may persist throughout adulthood.

Children who experience a divorce may exhibit separation anxiety, overly cling to other adults, or possibly develop reactive attachment disorder, a mental health condition marked by chronic difficulties forming and sustaining strong relationships with others, poor emotional regulation, and withdrawal from social engagement.

### 5. Behavioral Issues

Children going through a divorce from their parents may exhibit behavioral problems, including impulsivity, temper tantrums, resistance, and stubbornness, arguing, and even violence. Children will act out to win their parents' attention in certain cases, especially if they aren't receiving enough positive attention. A strongly aggressive divorce is associated with increased levels of disobedience, violence, and criminality, particularly in older children and adolescents.

Children may adopt these behaviors due to watching their parents deal with frustration, especially with one another, which is one explanation for this. But we'll take a closer look at that later in another section.

6. **Changes in Eating and Sleeping Patterns**

Children may have difficulty maintaining their usual eating and sleeping patterns due to the disruptions to their routines and structures resulting from a divorce. Whereas earlier sleep and mealtime rituals may have supplied this regularity, a loss of structure—or variability between households—due to the divorce may cause disturbances in these areas. It's also possible that children's stress takes the form of difficulties with eating or sleeping, such as an inability to eat, overeating, sleeplessness, or oversleeping.

7. **Risky Behavior**

Children (especially teenagers) may engage in dangerous activities, including theft, drug usage, and unprotected sex, due to their parent's divorce.

This could happen because of a need for immediate satisfaction, diverting attention away from unpleasant feelings, or seeking approval and affection from others to satisfy demands that aren't being satisfied at home.

8. **Physical Ailment**

Since physical sickness is sometimes a symptom of emotional distress, you may discover that your child is experiencing more frequent health complaints both during and after the divorce of his or her parents. According to one study, there is a direct correlation between claims of everyday headaches in children and parental divorce (Schwartz, 2022).

9. **Guilt**

Even after being persuaded that it is not their fault, children may believe that parental divorce is their fault. When a child feels guilty, they could take tremendous measures to appease their parents, stay out of trouble, and perhaps even grow perfectionistic inclinations. A child who feels guilty all the time may be experiencing depression.

10. **Regression in Development**

Following a divorce, especially among younger children, regressive behaviors—such as bedwetting and thumb-sucking—may manifest. Thumb-sucking and other seemingly infantile actions may be an attempt by a child to self-soothe, in contrast to bedwetting, which is frequently a physical representation of worry and emotional suffering.

## Does Divorce Have Long-Term Effects on Children?

If a child doesn't get the support they require during and after the divorce process, they may be more likely to experience unfavorable long-term effects as adults, including anxiety and depression, difficulty forming close bonds with others, divorce, substance use disorders, and even health issues like obesity.

Even though divorce can also have long-term impacts on a child, having parents who are supportive and consistent can go a long way toward assisting children in adjusting to the changes that are brought about by the divorce.

Divorce may have several long-term repercussions on a child, such as (Schwartz, 2022):

- **Developing mental health issues**: Children with divorced parents are more likely to develop anxiety and depression than their peers from intact households.
- **Issues in interpersonal relationships**: Children who experience parental divorce may be more likely to experience insecure attachment patterns in the future and may even experience divorce in their adult relationships.
- **At the risk of substance use**: Children of divorce are more likely to engage in excessive drinking, have alcohol-related issues, develop lifelong alcohol dependency, and engage in lifetime alcohol abuse.
- **Physical health issues**: Compared to children from intact households, studies demonstrate that divorce increases a child's risk of obesity. Additionally, those who had a parental divorce as parents see their health as poorer.

It is impossible to overstate the significance of your role as a parent in assisting your children in adjusting to life after the divorce. As parents, we are in the best position to prevent or reduce the potentially severe adverse effects on our children; we need to comfort them and shower them with love and understanding as soon as the divorce is in motion. Do not wait or hesitate to start implementing your new family structure and rituals. If you can help them adjust within the first few weeks or months, it will only benefit them and prevent more severe issues later on.

## THAT FIRST YEAR

A child goes through a significant and frequently painful change when their parents' divorce. From the child's perspective, this is the same as their family breaking up. When notified about the impending divorce, many children experience various negative emotions, including sadness, anger, and anxiety. Additionally, they may have a difficult time understanding how the course of their lives may alter. The age of a child is another factor that plays into how they react to the new arrangements in their family.

When going through a divorce with children, it is necessary to consider how the split may influence their lives. This section will provide a quick overview of what children of various ages can grasp and how you may help smooth their adjustment following a divorce.

Here are the effects of divorce on your child according to their age group (Broadwell, 2022):

### Babies: Children From Birth to 18 Months Old

Even infants are impacted by divorce, despite what some people think. When babies are young, they may feel the conflict between their parents and the home. Still, they cannot understand what is causing it—babies may grow agitated and clingy, especially around unfamiliar individuals, and exhibit frequent emotional outbursts if the tension persists. They could also go backward or exhibit indicators of being behind in development.

### Easing Into the New Normal

By providing their child with a home free from emotional risk, divorcing parents may make the adjustment to their new life easier. Babies thrive on predictability and habit and find comfort in things they already know. Maintaining regular daily schedules, especially concerning eating and sleeping, is beneficial during and after a divorce. Your child should have access to their preferred toys or comforts, and you should take additional care to hold them and provide physical comfort. Get enough rest and ask for assistance from friends and family so that you can be aware while your child is awake. Your infant will appreciate your efforts.

### Toddlers: Children From 18 Months to 3 Years Old

Divorce might emotionally and psychologically affect children between 18 months and three years. When a child is a toddler, their primary attachment is to their parents; as a result, it can be challenging for them to accept and grasp any changes in their family life during this time. In addition, because toddlers tend to be self-absorbed, they could blame themselves for their parent's divorce. They may cry and demand more attention than normal, go back to sucking their thumbs, refuse to use the bathroom, become afraid of being left alone, and have problems falling asleep or staying asleep on their own.

### Easing Into the New Normal

To make the adjustment to living after a divorce easier for their children, parents should consider making their children's daily routines a top priority. Parents should collaborate to build consistent and predictable routines so their children can easily follow them. Also, be sure to give your child enough one-on-one time and positive reinforcement from reliable adults in their lives. If your child is old enough to communicate, talk to them about their emotions, read books with them, and reassure them that they are not to blame for the breakup of the family.

### Preschoolers: Children From 3 to 6 Years Old

Children between the ages of three and six often struggle to comprehend the notion of divorce, mostly due to the terrifying degree of unpredictability it carries. No matter how difficult the situation at home may be, preschoolers cannot comprehend the concept of divorce and do not want their parents to part ways.

Preschoolers, like toddlers, may mistakenly feel that they are ultimately to blame because their parents are no longer together. It's possible that they'll have emotions of apprehension about the future, that they'll bottle up their rage, that they'll have unsettling ideas or thoughts, or that they'll have recurring nightmares.

### Easing Into the New Normal

Parents should commit to modeling the attitude and behavior they wish to see in their children between the ages of three and six. This will assist in easing the process of divorce for children in this age range.

Preschoolers will mimic the moods and attitudes of their parents, so parents should approach the divorce honestly and openly while maintaining a positive attitude.

Children of this age need to feel comfortable and secure. Tell them they will see their other parent, too, and they will regularly visit the non-custodial parent. You can help them feel at ease by establishing a regular visitation schedule and ensuring it is followed without fail.

## Children Between the Ages of 6 and 11 Years Old

Children between these ages may experience feelings of abandonment as a result of their parent's divorce.

Younger children, notably those aged 5 to 8 years old, may be unable to comprehend the notion and may have the impression that their parents are divorcing them. They can be concerned that they'll lose any of their parents and have illusions about their parents reconnecting. They frequently have the misconception that they can “save” their parents' marriage.

Children aged eight to eleven are particularly vulnerable to forming allegiances with one parent over the other during a family conflict. By engaging in physical altercations with peers, hurling insults at the world, or showing signs of anxiety, unwillingness, or depression, they may vent their rage while blaming their parents for being cruel or selfish. Some children have physical symptoms as a direct result of their parent's decision to divorce, such as headaches, upset stomachs, and even fabricated illnesses to avoid attending school.

## Easing Into the New Normal

By providing their children with opportunities to spend quality time together on a regular and dependable basis, divorcing parents may reduce the likelihood that their children will experience feelings of abandonment (Broadwell, 2022).

During a divorce, elementary-school children may experience great loss and rejection. Still, parents may help their children regain their security and sense of worth. The child should first spend meaningful time with each parent, encouraging them to talk about their feelings. Remind them that divorce is not their fault and neither parent will leave them. Likewise, parents must acknowledge that their decision to separate was mutual rather than placing blame on one another. Additionally, keeping a regular visitation schedule is crucial since children want stability, especially during turbulent times.

Finally, encourage your children to participate in activities that they find rewarding. At this age, academics, social relationships, and extracurricular pursuits all grow significantly. Encourage them to reach out to people rather than shutting themselves off from the world, and assist them in reviving their sense of self-worth.

## MY CHILD'S BEHAVIOR

It is not unusual for children to exhibit some behavioral issues following a divorce or separation. It's not surprising that a child would act out after a divorce or separation; it's a difficult time for the whole family.

Children often lack the emotional maturity to comprehend why they are being separated from their parents, depending on their ages and other conditions. As a result, their dissatisfaction and stress may show up in behavioral changes.

Children who have experienced divorce may exhibit various behavioral problems, from mild outbursts to extreme destructiveness. Ultimately, it is up to both mom and dad to keep an eye on their children's behavior, communicate with them, be patient, and ask a professional for assistance if the behavioral problems seem to be a sign of something more serious.

Here's what you need to know about your child's behavior (*Behavioral Issues in Children after Divorce*, 2023):

## Awareness and Preventive Measures

After a child's parents divorce or split, it is not unusual for the child to exhibit behavior problems of some kind. As a result of the things that are going on in your child's life, they may experience a range of feelings, including rage, confusion, frustration, and sadness. This emotional roller coaster is something that your child may go through. You can take measures to keep an eye on your child's behavior as well as your own, even though you have no control over how they feel about your divorce or separation.

## Keep an Eye Out for Worrying Signs, Such as Hostility or Depression, and Pay Attention to How They Manifest

Talk to your child's teachers, coaches, and any other adults who see your child outside of the home to get an accurate picture of their conduct while they are away from the house. Keeping a journal of your children's actions and, thus, any particular difficulties that you observe is an excellent method to record and recall what has been occurring recently and may become vital information to discuss with a professional when you discover a certain problematic behavior repeats.

Constant communication with your co-parent about your

child's behavior is essential. It's not uncommon for one parent to see one set of behaviors at home and the other to observe another. Recognizing how your child reacts to the various environmental stresses is crucial to providing appropriate assistance and support.

## Be Conscious of the Actions You Choose to Take

You must keep a close eye on how you act when you are in the presence of your child if you are a parent who is divorced, separated, or has visitation rights.

You can significantly affect your child's outlook on life and the world around them through your words and deeds. A child's feelings, outlook, and behavioral problems can all be easily influenced by certain behaviors, such as criticizing your ex-partner or moping in sadness in front of them.

If you're having difficulty keeping your emotions in check, acknowledge the fact and take the necessary steps to alleviate your distress. Remember that your children are watching and learning from your every move as you deal with your own feelings and those of your children.

## Adjusting the Course of Action

It is in your best interest to deal with the matter as quickly as possible if your child is beginning to display undesirable behavioral patterns. Many co-parents harbor guilt about the divorce, and this remorse may cause them to excuse specific actions taken by their children after their divorce. But allowing these behaviors to continue unchecked can make your child's mental and physical health worse in the long run, so you should avoid doing so.

## Supporting Children in Developing Their Emotional Intelligence

Children aren't always able to articulate the reasoning behind their decisions regarding their behavior. Understanding your internal motives is a skill that develops through time and with maturation; hence, it is not always possible for young children, in particular, to achieve this level of comprehension.

However, being able to discuss your emotions is a skill that can be learned, and parents can assist their children in developing this ability at a young age with their guidance. Helping your child better grasp how their behavior is related to their emotions may be accomplished by conversing with them and allowing them to talk openly and honestly about those feelings.

Parents need to talk to one another about the methods they use to discipline their children in both of their homes and the follow-up conversations they have with their children about the experience. Discuss what you have seen and decide together whether or not the behavior your child is displaying right now is something that you believe they will outgrow as they get older or not. It is likely time to seek assistance if you have seen patterns of behavior in your child that are troubling to you, your co-parent, and other people involved in your child's life.

For many families, behavioral problems in children following a separation or divorce are a complicated and frequent reality. However, there are methods that parents may cooperate with to help improve the situation for everyone concerned. When your child's behavior changes, it's essential to keep an eye on your feelings, have open conversations with them, exercises patience, and know when to seek professional help. After a divorce, controlling your behavior is one of the most important things to focus on. Focus on finding solutions to the issues you're facing right now so that more significant and intractable ones don't arise down the road.

### What Behavior Can I Expect From My Child?

During the process of divorce, children frequently act out. Certain behaviors are more visible than others, meaning you can miss some subtle changes in your child if you aren't actively searching for them. It should not come as a surprise that anything like this may occur.

When getting a divorce, you may feel that the world is moving extremely quickly and that you are battling to keep up. Rebuilding your life, your house, and even your job can be part of the process of getting a divorce, which must be done while simultaneously negotiating the end of your marriage. As a result, it may be pretty easy to lose track of how well your children are doing academically.

Divorce may profoundly impact children, increasing their risk for behavioral, mental health, and academic difficulties. As a result, addressing difficulties your children encounter as soon as they become noticeable is crucial. These effects may be long-lasting and continue to influence children even when they are adults. The crucial step is to recognize these changes.

You should keep an eye out for the following seven behaviors that your children may exhibit during the time that you are going through a divorce (Buie, 2021):

### 1. Engaging in Disruptive Behavior

Before you decided to get a divorce, your child might have been academically successful and respectful toward authoritative adults. But your child is no longer doing well academically and has suddenly developed behavioral issues at school. Your child may need assistance interacting with other children at school. Or maybe your child has started throwing tantrums or has started to argue with their sibling more violently than they have in the past.

Children who have been through a divorce often display traditional characteristics, like acting out. It almost always indicates that your child is attempting to attract your attention and will do whatever is possible. It is often essential to make a deliberate effort to check in with your child to make sure that they are getting the right amount of emotional care and attention from you since they must adjust to the fact that their parents are no longer in a relationship and the reality that you are busy coping with your divorce.

To do this, you should give some thought to creating a mental note that will serve as a daily reminder to engage in an authentic conversation with your children during the day when both of you are free from the interruptions of other activities.

If you really must, add the event to your calendar. An excellent time to connect with someone is typical during activities such as meals, vehicle rides, or before bed. Keep going if you receive an answer the first time you attempt. It may take time to pull down the barriers your child has constructed.

### 2. **An Unexpected Change in Weight, Either an Increase or a Loss**

Individuals struggling emotionally may resort to various coping mechanisms, such as food. There is no difference between children and adults.

Children may turn to food for the peace and comfort they need when their parents argue over their divorce. Alternatively, your child may stop eating because of the stress and negative feelings they are experiencing due to your divorce.

Your child may have numerous physical and emotional health issues as a result of having a disordered connection. Be aware of what your children are taking into their bodies, and pay attention to it.

### 3. **Severe Shifts in Mood or Frequent Outbursts of Negative Feelings**

If your child has frequent mood swings, tantrums, or fits of uncontrollable sobbing, they may be struggling to deal with their emotions as a result of your divorce. If your child was previously peaceful and well-behaved but has recently acquired these habits, speak to your physician.

### 4. **Pretending to Be Sick**

Your child, who previously had a flawless or almost perfect attendance record at school, suddenly complains of feeling unwell almost frequently. Whether it's an upset stomach, a headache, or some other sickness that defies description, it's preventing your child from participating in a fundamental aspect of their development.

Your child may pretend to be sick to obtain more attention from you. Another possibility is that it is a symptom of their depression. In either case, you should address the issue as soon as possible before it has a compounding effect and causes the individual to fall farther behind in academics, lose friendships, or become sad.

### 5. **Sleeping Issues**

When coping with significant stress or emotional upheaval, your regular sleeping routine may be disrupted. This also applies to young children.

If your child, who used to be able to fall asleep effortlessly and stay asleep all night, is having difficulty accomplishing either of these things or would prefer to sleep in your bedroom with you. If that's the case, they could feel stressed about your upcoming divorce. Your child could want to sleep in the same bed as you at night to make up for the fact that during the day, they weren't getting the same degree of comfort and security.

There is no denying that this conduct is harmful to them; nevertheless, it is also possible for it to be harmful to you. To stay strong for yourself and your child, you must maintain a nighttime sleep routine free of interruptions.

### 6. **Displaying a Different Demeanor When Interacting With the Other Parent**

When a child goes from living in a family with one household to living in a family with two households, especially if one of the parents moves away from the family home to live somewhere else, the child may feel abandoned and act out against one or both parents.

A divorce is a difficult process, and children, particularly younger children, may not have the cognitive ability to comprehend the complexities of your marriage. They don't see you as the husband and wife struggling to make their marriage work; they see you as their mom and dad.

You want your child to have healthy relationships with you and the other parent, even if you no longer live together. Suppose your child begins to behave differently when spending time with one of you. In that case, it is crucial to intervene and help your child better grasp the changes that have taken place in the family setting. Help is available from mental health professionals.

### 7. Refusing to Adhere to Their Schedule

Children often adhere to a schedule that includes school, extracurricular activities, and homework. They depend on it for stability and even yearn for it.

So, let's say your child starts disobeying you and breaking your rules due to the divorce. You may be experiencing this due to the many emotional challenges your divorce has caused.

Your child may feel that they've lost all power in their lives and that the schedule is the only thing they have any say over. Sometimes, they do not want to carry on with their routine because they are depressed.

Your child may experience difficulties in school, emotionally, and socially if they do not adhere to a schedule. The reasons for this may vary. From that point on, problems are only going to get worse.

The best course of action for you to take is to maintain a cautious eye while continuing your previous level of active involvement with your child after the divorce. Or, if the situation calls for it, elevate your game. The best way to reassure your children that you will always be there for them is to demonstrate that you will.

*How can I help my child get through this stronger?*

The following chapter examines how you can calm your child's fears about divorce, teach them about their emotions, and explain why seeking professional help is worthwhile.

# CHAPTER 5: HOW CAN I SUPPORT MY CHILD?

Even though children's reactions to their parent's divorce are typically quite diverse from one another, they all require regular care, room to process their feelings, and affirmation. Think about setting aside a certain amount of time to have a conversation with your child regarding the divorce, their perspective on it, and how it made them feel.

Remember that you should respect their boundaries, even if they are unwilling to do so themselves. If they are willing to discuss their sentiments with you, validate them by saying things like "It makes sense that you..." or "I can imagine you're experiencing..."

You must keep a close eye on how much information you share with your child regarding your divorce and how you feel about your former partner. Self-compassion, support, and counseling can minimize the probability that your child will carry the divorce's weight.

It's essential to remember that there are good outcomes for

children if they are adequately supported during a divorce, such as living in a healthier family, witnessing their parents happier, spending more time with their parents one-on-one, and learning that change is difficult but can be overcome.

## HOW TO CALM YOUR CHILD'S FEARS AFTER THE DIVORCE

You can make your child feel better about your decision to split up. In what ways do you believe your child has been affected by the fact that you divorced? They may have only known about the idea and process through TV shows or stories from friends. Whether the idea is well-established or not, it is understandable for a child to have concerns about what divorce would entail for their family. You, as parents, can dispel these worries before they have an even more negative effect on your child.

Here are some frequent concerns children have after learning their parents are divorcing and how you might soothe them (*How to Debunk Your Child's Post-Divorce Fears*, 2023):

### 1. My Parents Despise One Another

When you and your other co-parent have had a significant disagreement due to your divorce, your child might worry that this fighting has produced rifts in their family that can never be repaired. Children may witness tense conflicts, see improper texts, or overhear their parents disparaging one another when communication is not handled appropriately. In turn, this can make them think that their parents will always fight. Suppose the fight spreads to other family members. In that case, it could make the children worry about how they get along with their aunts, uncles, and grandparents.

As you become more comfortable with co-parenting, disagreements may arise. However, as long as you have a parental plan in place and are also using tools to help you deal with conflict, your children will see a much better example of how to deal with disagreements while remaining confident in their connections with both of their parents.

### 2. "I'll Have to Pick One Parent Over the Other"

Because parenting schedules are elaborate affairs that, even for adults, can sometimes be perplexing, it is not surprising that children might grow anxious about the long-term effects that these schedules will have on their families. Some children could even be concerned about having to decide between their parents. These fears can worsen if the other parent makes them feel bad when they say they miss one parent.

A child should never feel like they have to choose between their parents. Even though you and your co-parent may no longer talk to each other, your child may still talk to them. If your child says, they miss the other parent, respond positively. If your child shows concerns about the time they'll spend with the other parent, be careful that any hatred you may have toward your co-parent does not come out in your response. It's normal for children to miss their parents. The more comfortable your child is talking about both of their houses, the less anxious they will be while switching between them.

### 3. "It's My Fault That They're Splitting Up"

Children often blame themselves for the breakup of a relationship because they can't understand why grown-up relationships end. This fear can make children of every age feel bad about themselves and change how they see themselves.

Many different approaches may be taken to alleviate the anxiety that children experience. Since this is a widespread worry, many books and other resources are available to help children of all ages cope with this terrible idea. Sharing the news of your divorce with your co-parent is another way to ease your children's minds. Let them ask you questions, and when you answer, be honest. The more they know about your breakup, at least the age-appropriate parts, the less likely they are to blame themselves for their sadness.

When children hear that their parents are splitting up, it's normal for them to feel anxious or worried. Still, parents willing to work together can calm many of their fears. Parents won't be able to stop their children from experiencing every single worry or fear. Divorce is never easy, but talking to your children about the worries that come up during this time can show them that you care and support them as they navigate any difficult feelings they may be experiencing.

## HOW TO TEACH MY CHILD ABOUT THEIR FEELINGS

Even for adults, emotions may be difficult to navigate, let alone for a four-year-old who doesn't grasp why they can't have another cookie or an eight-year-old who is disappointed that their day at the playground will end early because their parents have to go to work.

Because sentiments are such abstract notions, explaining them to young children can be challenging. It is difficult to describe what it is like to be sad, terrified, or excited. It is critical to begin educating children about their feelings at the earliest possible age since children's sentiments influence every decision they make.

Children with a healthy understanding of their feelings are far less likely to behave negatively, such as by throwing tantrums, being aggressive, or being defiant. Children who communicate their emotions are less likely to resort to physical aggression. A child who can articulate their distress by stating, "That makes me feel..." is better prepared to negotiate a peaceful resolution to a confrontation.

Your child's development as a mentally robust adult will be aided by your teaching them about their feelings. Children who have a solid understanding of their feelings and are equipped with the coping mechanisms necessary to manage them will have the self-assurance to know that they can overcome any challenge that life may provide.

Here's how you can help children understand their emotions (Morin, 2020):

### 1. **Label the Emotions**

Teach your child simple descriptors for emotions, including joyful, furious, sad, and terrified. Learning more complicated words to describe feelings, such as irritated, disappointed, and nervous, might benefit older children.

Talking to children about the emotions that could be experienced by characters in stories or on television can be a fruitful method of teaching them about their feelings. Put a pause in the conversation to inquire, "How do you suppose he is feeling right now?" Next, you should talk about the many emotions that the character can be feeling and the causes behind those sentiments.

Teaching empathy also includes having conversations about the emotions of other people. To a young child, the world may seem to center on him or her alone, so it may be a shock to discover that other individuals also experience the full range of human emotions. Your child's likelihood of shoving their buddy to the ground will decrease if they are aware that their friend may get upset and angry due to the act.

### 2. **Talk About Feelings**

Teach children to incorporate words that describe their feelings into their everyday lexicon. Take advantage of the opportunity to talk about how you feel so that others can learn from your example. You might say, "I'm sorry that you chose not to consider sharing your toy with your brother today. I'm sure he's very sad, too."

Ask your child this daily question: “How are you feeling today?” If you have small children, you might find it helpful to create a basic chart with smiling faces so they can choose an emotion and then talk about that feeling together. Have a conversation with your child about the several factors that might affect their feelings.

Bring attention to the moments you have seen that your child is most likely experiencing a certain emotion. For instance, you might say, “You seem incredibly glad because we are going to be enjoying ice cream,” or you could remark, “It appears like you are becoming irritated playing with those blocks.” Both would be appropriate responses.

### 3. **Teach Coping Skills**

Children have a responsibility to learn that even if they feel furious, that does not allow them to hurt another person. Instead, individuals should develop skills for controlling their anger so that they may find peaceful solutions to conflicts. Instill in your child the skills necessary to cope with feelings that are difficult to experience.

You should encourage your children to take a timeout for themselves. When they feel unhappy, you should encourage them to retire to their room or some other location where they can be alone and quiet. They may find it easier to regain their composure if they do this before breaking a rule and being sent to timeout.

Teach your child positive coping mechanisms for dealing

with negative emotions such as sadness. Discuss strategies to cope with unhappy feelings with your child if they are experiencing them due to their friend's refusal to play with them. When children are unhappy, they frequently act out aggressively or in other ways designed to attract attention because they are at a loss for what to do.

4. **Provide Positive Reinforcement**

A positive consequence should reinforce appropriate behavior. Your child should be praised for expressing their feelings in a socially acceptable manner. You may say something to your child along the lines of, "I appreciate the way you used your words while you told your little sister that you were mad at her."

A reward system is another fantastic method that may promote healthy behaviors; it may encourage children to practice more constructive methods of coping with negative emotions, such as anger, rather than acting out aggressively.

5. **Set a Good Example With Your Choices**

When your child sees you hurling your phone across the room after a call doesn't go through, they won't believe you when you advise them to use their words. Set an example for others of how to deal constructively with difficult feelings.

Identify and express out loud the situations that cause you anger or frustration. You may say something like, "Wow, I'm upset that car just drove in front of me," for example. Then you should try taking a few deep breaths or modeling another healthy coping technique so that your child may learn to identify the abilities you use when you're upset and employ them themselves.

Throughout their childhood, including when they are teenagers, you will need to engage in emotional development work with your child. Maintaining a constant dialogue about how to deal with your feelings in a way that benefits your health is essential.

Consider it a chance to show your child how to do better the next time they make a mistake, lose patience, or smash something out of rage. Remember that there will be many opportunities to teach them valuable lessons as you guide them toward more adaptive coping mechanisms for dealing with difficult emotions.

### 6. Keep the Following in Mind

According to Schwartz (2022), parents can show their child(ren) support when going through a divorce in the following ways:

- **Motivating them to discuss their emotions openly**: Fostering emotional vulnerability, intimacy, and processing in children may be accomplished by ensuring they are aware it is safe to discuss how they feel without pressuring them to do so. This teaches children not to repress their feelings, which might lead to various difficulties related to mental health in the future.
- **Giving confidence to their emotions**: If you want to affirm what your child is experiencing, you don't need to agree with how they act or feel. To ensure that

children have feelings of love, support, and visibility, it is essential to reassure them that their emotions are reasonable and warranted.

- **Keeping the relational issues that you and your partner are experiencing separate**: It's natural to want to talk about how you feel about your relationship, and it's also natural to want to defend your decision to break up with them. However, it is essential that children not be exposed to knowledge about relationship issues that are irrelevant to them since this might put them in danger of experiencing an emotional injury.
- **Modeling self-compassion is important since children pick up on habits that are exemplified for them**: As a result, teaching children how to be kind and nonjudgmental is essential. One strategy for achieving this goal is to instruct the individual in self-soothing. Try expressing something like, "I'm having a terrible day today," for example. I feel that I need to go outdoors and see a beautiful sunset. Would you be interested in coming with me?

When parents take care of their mental health, it benefits their children, who also fare better. Putting yourself first will assist your child's mental health, despite what can seem paradoxical. You can accomplish this goal by participating in psychotherapy, employing coping strategies, establishing a routine, and participating in activities that please you.

## When to Seek the Assistance of a Professional

It is not uncommon for children to experience emotional and behavioral difficulties after their parents' divorce. If, on the other hand, they express a desire for you to seek the assistance of a counselor or other mental health professional, or if the problematic conduct continues despite your efforts to address it, you could decide.

Play and cognitive behavioral therapy (also known as CBT) are two types of individual therapy that are realistic possibilities for providing your child with the necessary one-on-one care from a trained practitioner. Family counseling could also help address more significant systemic issues that affect families. Your child may also benefit from connecting with other children their age and exploring their emotions in a safe and supportive setting by participating in support or process groups. Consider having a conversation with the physician or guidance counselor at your child's school if you need clarification on how to get started.

## New Beginnings

The emotional roller coaster ride for children does not stop with the divorce. They must continue to attend therapy sessions to assist them in adjusting to the new *normal* that is gradually forming in their lives due to the formal separation. Having a communication channel and emotional support from a counselor may be a source of stability and comfort that helps our children cope with the new changes to their family circumstances, as these changes can cause ripples of disturbance across their social life, schoolwork, and also their continuous development of identity (Wake Forest University, 2017).

The emotional and relational assistance couples and families receive from marital and family therapists while dissolving a marriage is beneficial years afterward. Especially if transitioning from a two-parent family to a single-parent household, parents might benefit from assistance in developing the skills necessary to effectively communicate with and care for their children by channeling the love and compassion they feel for their children into actionable skills. Changes in child custody may be complex for everyone involved, including the child and his or her parents. These changes can impact relationships, rules, and financial assistance for the child's education. As families continue to develop and adapt, counselors may assist in closing the gap between the past and the present and offer enduring insight.

When it comes to assisting children in coping with the news, the process, and the aftermath of a divorce, the role of counselors is significant.

## On Becoming Mentally Strong

*What exactly does your child need to thrive, regardless of the situation they might find themselves in?*

The following chapter will examine the importance of cultivating a strong mentality, raise some critical questions on what you think your child needs, and provide practical steps on how you can teach them the skills they need going forward.

# CHAPTER 6: WHAT THEY NEED TO THRIVE

If you want to be a practical guide and nurturer for your child throughout their growth and maturity, one of the essential things you can do is learn about your child and come to terms with the fact that he or she has distinct personality traits that will remain constant throughout their lives.

You may better understand your child by watching them when they are sleeping, eating, or playing and looking for repeated patterns of behavior. What kinds of things do they enjoy doing the most? Do they readily adapt to new circumstances, or do they require more time to grow accustomed to other things?

It is essential to acquire knowledge and build an understanding of your children; therefore, devote as much time as possible to having conversations with them as often as possible. When it comes to young children, it is necessary to rely more on their facial expressions and body language to grasp their thoughts and emotions than their verbal language. If you ask them questions, it will be easier for your children to communicate their thoughts and feelings.

The cultivation of a good self-concept as well as a healthy sense of self-esteem, is essential to one's achievement in life. It is vital to the fulfillment and accomplishments of children and adolescents. A child's development of self-respect and social responsibility is greatly aided by the stability and love they get from their parents. Because spending time with us helps them feel loved and cared for, our children strongly desire to spend more time with us.

Some children, for whatever reason(s), cannot develop their social skills to the same extent as others. They may sincerely cultivate relationships with their peers, only to be met with rejection or even outright abuse, prompting them to seek refuge in the protection of their homes and families and the companionship of only themselves.

Perhaps nothing causes a parent to feel as much anguish as when their child is rejected. Parents are responsible for evaluating issues about their children's social lives with the same level of caution and forethought as they do issues about their children's academic performance or physical well-being.

This chapter will look at how you can help your child nurture their sense of self, teach them to become mentally tough, learn what skills they need to become more resilient and support them in developing emotionally strong individuals.

## NURTURE YOUR CHILD'S SELF-CONCEPT

Self-concept is how people think about themselves and what they can do. At birth, a child starts to learn about himself or herself. It all starts with how adults treat them. Through warm and kind interactions, parents and other caregivers can build a healthy emotional connection with a newborn. A secure emotional connection with caring adults is important for a child's developing a good sense of identity.

*Why is it important to help my child establish a sense of self-esteem?*

A recent study found that children's self-esteem was the most important element in determining how positively or negatively they responded to the traumatic experience of their parents' divorce (Fisher, 2019). Children with low self-esteem are more likely to have worse "adjustment" (coping) throughout their lives for every trauma they experience due to their parent's divorce. Children are active in dealing with problems, and self-esteem is a big part of this. Previous studies have shown that children with a healthy belief in themselves are more likely to get compliments and encouragement from adults. Children of divorce don't just have lives with their parents. They also have lived with their extended families, their friends, and at school. A child can overcome trauma at home by having successful experiences in various other areas.

As a child grows, being able to interact well with their surroundings helps them develop a healthy sense of self. This is very important for young children. Having a good idea of oneself from a young age gives a child the confidence to try new things, feel good about themselves, and try to do well. As parents, we are tasked with the opportunity and the obligation to help our children develop healthy self-concepts.

How can parents promote a healthy sense of self in their children?

- **Think about the words you use to talk about your children**: Do not use words like *lazy, bad, aggressive,* or *mean* to describe them. Instead, look for your child's strengths and point them out.
- **Give them chances to be successful**: Give your child tasks that are right for their age and that she can do independently. This will make them proud of themselves and help them develop a *can-do* attitude.
- **Show your children that you believe in them**: This has to do with the language used. For instance, if your toddler lashes out at another child because they

are frustrated, you may reprimand them by saying, "You *bad* girl!" Why are you so mean? I'm shocked that you hit him! You are in a lot of trouble!" You could also say, "You were angry and hit him. Hitting is not okay. I know it wasn't your intention to hurt him. How can you show how upset you are in different ways?"

- **Spend time together**: Having a healthy view of yourself means feeling loved and important. During your time together, you should do something that the two of you will find pleasurable, and you should avoid giving each other criticism or giving lectures.
- **Show interest in what your child likes**: Find out what they enjoy doing and help them develop the necessary skills or reach their goals. A reasonable opinion of yourself grows when you feel good about something and are competent at it; it works the same for your child.
- **Make rules that make sense and follow them with kindness**: Your guidelines must be age-appropriate and easy to understand. Your child will learn to feel protected and will have the ability to manage themselves with this support. But disciplining your child harshly when they break the rules can hurt their sense of self-worth. It's important to teach your child that making mistakes is normal and doesn't make them bad people. Keep your child's pride in mind when giving consequences.
- **Teach your child how to effectively regulate their feelings and find solutions to difficulties they might face**: Solving problems is important to being a

good parent. Children develop confidence and a healthy sense of self-worth when they are taught to resolve their challenges. Emotional control is essential for objectivity.

- **Stay connected**: Maintaining connections ensures that communication channels are kept open, which is the greatest priority when your child enters adolescence. It will be easier for them to feel supported, protected, and necessary if they know they can talk to you, that you will listen to what they say without passing judgment on it right away, and that you will take their feelings seriously.
- **Allow them to explore their surroundings**: Encourage them to ask questions without making them feel like they're being bothersome, and let them participate in pretend play activities. Children are naturally curious and creative, and we shouldn't try to stop them from being that way. To encourage curiosity and creativity, give children a lot of time to play and explore independently.
- **Express gratitude and support for efforts**: Children must understand that coming in first place is not the purpose of competitions but that doing one's best is a victory, regardless of where it places them. Self-evaluation will become increasingly significant to their identity as they mature; they'll need to learn to value and highlight their qualities and successes, even if they don't get a medal for their efforts.

A child's positive growth and well-being depend on how he or she feels about himself or herself. When a child has a good self-concept, he views himself as being cherished, loved, and valued; this is something we all desire for our children. Thus, they must develop a healthy sense of themselves as they grow.

Equally important is teaching them how to become mentally strong in adversity.

## HOW YOUR CHILD CAN HAVE A MENTALLY STRONG ATTITUDE

Children who have developed their mental strength are better able to meet the demands of adulthood. Mental toughness does not consist of appearing tough or repressing one's feelings. Furthermore, being cruel or acting defiantly is not the point here. Instead, children with mental toughness are taught to be resilient and demonstrate the courage and confidence to achieve their maximum potential. There are things that you, as a parent, can teach them to assist in the process of helping them cultivate and creating mental toughness in your children.

Children who have developed a strong mental capacity are better equipped to solve issues, recover from setbacks, and persevere in adversity (Morin, 2015). A three-pronged strategy is required to assist children in the development of mental toughness.

There are a variety of approaches to parenting, methods of discipline, and educational resources that can assist children in developing their mental strength. Adjust your strategy so that it takes into account the particular requirements of your child.

The following section will serve as a guide on how to help your child become mentally strong (Morin, 2015):

## Teach Your Children How to Be Brave

Showing children how to live their lives might be one of the most effective methods to educate them on mental strength. Children learn how to react to various scenarios by observing how their parents handle them. To enhance your mental fortitude, you must be aware of where you stand and teach them accordingly.

Some suggestions for teaching your children the value of emotional and mental resilience (Morin, 2015):

### 1. Mental Strength Should Be Modeled

The most effective strategy to assist your child in becoming mentally strong is to set a good example. Discuss your aspirations for the future with your child and demonstrate that you are making efforts to become more capable. Focus on your self-improvement and mental toughness as a top goal, and steer clear of the activities that mentally strong parents would never engage in.

### 2. Demonstrate to Your Child the Art of Confronting Fears

Your child won't develop the self-assurance they need to deal with uncomfortable feelings if they stay away from anything that makes them scared. Help your child take baby steps toward conquering their anxieties, whether they are afraid of the dark or interacting with strangers.

They will realize they are capable individuals who can manage to be outside their comfort zone if they are encouraged during the experience, praised for their efforts, and rewarded for their bravery.

*How can I help cultivate my child's social skills?*

## How to Raise a Child Who Is Socially Intelligent

Your child navigates a highly complex social environment. This has always been the case for children: all parents can recall their tears or wrath at the harsh behavior of this other child, and most parents can recall their immense desire to be loved and accepted by other children. Most of us can recall a time when we yearned for a close confidante or companion.

The media exposed children to adult norms before they were emotionally mature, making things much more challenging for them today. In a world of shifting regulations, our children do not automatically know how to form positive relationships with other children.

Fortunately, healthy children typically make good decisions when challenged by peers. Children get a great head start if they have positive interactions at home. However, they still want your assistance in figuring out how to function in a complicated social environment.

Some fundamentals for assisting children in acquiring the necessary social skills:

- **Develop social abilities from a young age**: This is among the most crucial skill sets your children will ever develop. It is far more crucial to their future happiness than supporting their intellectual growth.

- **Encourage friendships**: Respect and support your child's growing friendships. Create chances to play, remember them, and talk about them. Remember that just like adults, children can grow frustrated with one another. It doesn't always indicate that a friendship is over; it just means that they require assistance to resolve the problems that arise.
- **Set a good example for respectful relationships**: Remember that your children will treat others as they are treated, so model positive behavior for them. Not only does this include treating them politely daily, but it also necessitates delivering constructive criticism to them behind closed doors and away from the public.
- **Teach your child the value of people**: All parents must pick and choose which fights to fight, so if you must, put up with the messiness and tardiness while teaching your child to show concern for others. Encourage it, set a good example for your child, assist them in developing creative solutions to peer conflicts, and ensure your child never consciously or unconsciously disrespects anybody. Make sure to bring it up later if you can't face it immediately without making your child uncomfortable. As children get older, you need to be extremely clear when you demand that they acknowledge other children as well as adults who are there. It is common for preteens and early teenagers to require a reminder of this fact and guidance on managing social situations that make them uncomfortable.
- **Teach children how to communicate their desires and needs without being rude to others**: Instead of

saying, "You're nasty," say, "I dislike it whenever you push right in front of us like that." Instead of saying, "You're hoarding the ball," say, "I could use a turn, too."

- **Foster the ability in your child to mend connections**: Usually, when we consider how to mend a relationship, we concentrate on apologizing. Premature apologies, however, won't be sincere, and they risk making the child harbor resentment. It always works better if you give them time to calm down first. People in our society find it challenging to apologize, mainly because we believe it proves we are terrible or incorrect for making the error in the first place. However, it is an essential friendship skill. However, the conflict will inevitably arise in human interactions, and children need help developing their conflict management skills. Therefore, avoid turning your child's apology into a public humiliation, or they will always reject it. Additionally, make sure you're modeling apologies. They won't if you never say you're sorry. If you apologize to them and others in a kind manner and do so frequently, others will follow your example. Making an apology into a reward is not the key to teaching children to apologize.

*How else can I help my child develop a stronger mentality?*

## Developing Mental Toughness is the Goal

Always look for opportunities to teach your children how to be psychologically resilient. As you interact with children in various contexts, you can help them develop the emotional and mental resilience they'll need to succeed in adversity.

Here are some concrete steps you can take to provide your children with the mental fortitude to handle whatever the future may bring (Morin, 2015):

1. **Develop Particular Skills**

Instead of punishing your children for their transgressions, discipline should focus on teaching them how to improve in the future. Use consequences that teach concrete abilities like problem-solving, self-control, and self-discipline. Your child will be able to learn how to act constructively by utilizing these abilities, even when confronted with temptation, challenging situations, and challenging failures.

2. **Emotion Regulation Skills**

When your child is upset, don't try to soothe them; when they're depressed, don't try to cheer them up. Instead, you should instruct them on how to cope with unsettling feelings all on their own so that they do not come to rely on you to keep their moods in check. Children who are aware of their emotions and have developed coping mechanisms are better equipped to handle difficult situations.

Children and adults of all ages may better manage their emotional reactions using emotional regulation skills. Young children who acquire these skills are better prepared to deal with challenging emotions and overcome obstacles in life. Children must experiment to see what works best for them, just as with other talents. Children can add the following abilities to their *emotional toolkits*:

Following are some suggestions for assisting your children in learning to control their feelings (Stone, 2022):

- **Name the emotion**: Children who can identify their emotions and express them to you are better equipped to control those emotions and receive the appropriate support when they do. With the use of feeling words, parents may help their young children comprehend and express the many feelings they experience. Although mastering this ability may be challenging, it is essential if you want to help your child get through the difficult period. Give your child a statement with gaps they can fill in, such as "I feel _______ when _______," if they need additional help.
- **Focus on your body**: children can also work on tuning into their bodies and observing the bodily sensations accompanying certain emotions. Children's comprehension of the mind-body link and how our emotions affect our bodies will develop as they practice self-awareness. Sometimes it's enough to acknowledge your feelings and use self-control to get through them. Children may use this interesting body map to illustrate where they experience *hot* and *cold* emotions in their bodies.
- **Pause**: Children can learn to pause inside before responding to challenging emotions. Similar to how you would stop a movie by using the pause button. This coping mechanism can aid children with self-

control and reduce temper outbursts. Children can control their emotions and select what to do next when there is a time between a feeling and a response. This is a good opportunity to apply a regulating or coping method to reevaluate your emotions.

- **Use a relaxation technique or coping mechanism**: Using coping mechanisms like deep breathing and relaxation methods might help us maintain emotional control when experiencing strong emotions that could result in meltdowns.
- **Self-care**: Self-care is our routine action to maintain health and balance. Maintaining emotional control is much simpler when we're at our best. Remember that children observe their role models and learn a lot from them about how to handle situations. It sets a terrific example if you put your mental health and self-care first. Have your youngster develop a list of the things that give them joy and energy. Both require understanding what makes you happy and how to deal with difficult emotions, which are crucial. It's vital for many reasons to learn how to manage and express your feelings. Learning to control one's emotions is essential for maintaining physical, mental, and spiritual wellness.

3. **Allow Your Child to Learn From Their Mistakes**

If you want your child to learn without feeling bad about making mistakes, you need to help them understand that making mistakes is a natural part of the learning process. Allow for the natural repercussions when it is safe to do so, and then discuss ways to prevent making the same error again.

## Cultivate Resilient Skills

To develop children's mental capacity, focus on boosting their self-esteem and confidence and encouraging their sense of autonomy. Help your children improve these aspects of their lives while encouraging them to develop healthy routines that will strengthen their minds.

Here are some ways that children might expand on the knowledge that they are gaining about mental toughness (Morin, 2015):

### 1. **Encourage Positive Self-Talk**

When children constantly criticize or tear themselves down or anticipate the worst possible consequences, it can be challenging for them to have a sense of mental strength. You should teach your child how to reframe unfavorable views, so they think more rationally. Children can improve their ability to strive through challenging circumstances and reach their full potential if they cultivate a perspective that is both realistic and hopeful.

2. **Develop Character**

To guide them toward more wholesome choices, today's youth require a strong moral compass. Put in a lot of effort to ensure your child inherits your ideals. Regularly put yourself in situations where you learn valuable lessons that will help you uphold your principles. For instance, instead of emphasizing winning at any cost, highlight the significance of being honest and compassionate.

Children who have a clear understanding of their own beliefs and principles are much more likely to make decisions that are beneficial to their health, even when the acts they do conflict with the beliefs and principles of others.

3. **Allow Your Child Freedom to Experience Uncomfortable Feelings**

It may be tempting to step in and assist a child anytime they are having difficulty, yet doing so would just teach the child that they are powerless if they are rescued from their predicament. Allow your child to make mistakes, let them become bored, and demand that they take responsibility even if they don't want to. Your child can develop mental resilience by working through challenges while receiving support and direction.

The earlier children can acquire conflict resolution skills, the sooner they may develop emotional intelligence, which is important for tolerating others and preventing conflicts.

Children can learn to resolve disputes independently using the following model (Engler, 2022):

- **Stop**: Prevent things from spinning out of control. Try to take a deep breath and relax; anger just worsens things.
- **Say**: What is the problem at hand? Verify that you and your partner have a firm grasp on the issue, and define your individual needs and objectives specifically.
- **Think**: Which favorable alternatives are there? What's a fair way to solve the problem that works for both of you?
- **Choose**: What is a choice that is favorable to everyone?
- **Respect**: Teach children to respect other people's opinions, even if they disagree with them.

### 4. Make Gratitude One of Your Top Priorities

Gratefulness is good therapy for self-pity and other negative behaviors that might impede your child from developing strong mental health. Assist your child in recognizing the many reasons they have to be grateful for, even when they feel the most oppressed, by pointing out the many positive things in the world. Your child's attitude can be improved, as can their ability to be proactive, by practicing gratitude.

### 5. Recognizing and Accepting Personal Responsibility

Accepting one's responsibility is necessary to build mental strength. When your child misbehaves or makes a mistake, it is okay to offer explanations but never excuses. If you see that your child is trying to blame others for their thoughts, feelings, or actions, you should correct them.

Commitment and consistency are the most critical factors when developing your child's mental power. You will be able to instill mental toughness in them if you communicate with them consistently, put them in challenging circumstances where they can practice what they have learned, and consistently try to boost their confidence and self-esteem.

Try to find possibilities, begin with a limited scope, and then expand. In addition to that, you should assist them in developing and learning from their errors. Your children will only spend time building up mental fortitude that will serve them well for the rest of their lives.

### Important Questions to Consider

It's easy for parents who are absorbed in the divorce drama to lose sight of their children's basic emotional and security requirements. The following questions and remarks should remind you of your child's essential requirements for psychological well-being. Give these questions some thought, and give yourself some time to respond.

These are the essential questions to ponder (Brady, 2013):

#### 1. How Can I Encourage My Child to Feel Secure and Confident in Themselves, Other People, and the World and Be Able to Meet Their Needs?

A sense of family and being loved are essential for a child's development. They must feel significant and understand that aid is available. That their requirements will be taken into account... believe there are moral principles to follow, in addition to virtues like justice, compassion, courage, and honesty.

### 2. How Can I Prevent My Child From Witnessing and Experiencing Too Many Arguments and Stresses at Home?

Adults can handle more than children can. A child needs to feel secure and protected at home. Be sure that a responsible party is in place and will prevent events or feelings of excessive intensity from happening. Will reasonably impose boundaries and listen with kindness. Help clarify perplexing circumstances to alleviate any concerns.

### 3. How Can I Assist My Child in Overcoming Shame and Guilt When They Make a Mistake, Get Hurt, or Fall Short of Their Goals?

Instead of feeling humiliated or penalized for making errors, children should learn from them. They must have self-confidence and understand that making mistakes is okay. And that you continue to love them and have faith in their abilities. They must understand that your divorce was not their fault, particularly at this time.

### 4. What Can I Do to Support and Boost My Child's Self-Esteem?

Children must understand that their value as people and as children comes from who they are, not just what they have accomplished. They must know that you will accept them no matter what, even if your behavior standards differ from those of others. Knowing that both of their parents adore them is crucial now. Since your child is a part of the other parent, criticizing that parent is like criticizing a portion of your child. Even if you are upset, refrain from criticizing the other parent.

### 5. **How Can I Help My Child Develop a Sense of Independence and Competence?**

In general, it is essential for children to feel as though they have accomplished something, even if doing so may make them incorrect or unique. For them to feel trustworthy and capable, they need to be able to manage specific tasks independently or with minimum help, have some control over their environment, and have access to options. Your child could get more frightened and return to an earlier developmental stage during the divorce. Recognize that your child may want to feel more like a "little child" than "Mommy's/Daddy's big boy/girl," and treat him or her with respect if this is the case. This should only be a temporary problem if it is treated with kindness. It can signify excessive emotional stress if it lasts a long time.

### 6. **How Do I Discipline My Children Without Making Them Feel Bad About Themselves?**

Simply put, you should restrict your child's actions, not their ideas or feelings. Thoughts and sentiments are not inherently *evil,* but behavior sometimes is. Make an effort to shape your thinking, comprehend and accept your emotions, and change your conduct. The concept of discipline should not be viewed as a kind of punishment but rather as an opportunity to impart important life lessons to one's child.

### 7. How Can I Encourage My Child to Have a Positive Self-Image, Whether Male or Female, to Feel Safe While Not With Me, and to Be Curious About the World?

To start answering the question "Who am I?" children need to acquire a sense of identity. They also need to learn that being themselves is satisfying. They will feel more confident in their self-discovery the more they feel loved, understood, and trusted. Your child will learn much about this through your example and interaction with them.

## The Next Step

The final section will help bring all the concepts together so that you can have peace of mind, knowing that even though co-parenting is not an easy task, the efforts you put in will be worth it at the end of the day.

# SECTION 3: HOW TO PRACTICE EFFECTIVE CO-PARENTING

The concluding section will guide you in reinforcing all that you've come to learn in this book, as well as how you can overcome the challenges associated with co-parenting and find balance in this seeming chaos.

# CHAPTER 7: POSSIBLE STUMBLING BLOCKS AHEAD

*How will my child respond to my new partner? Will my ex-partner and I ever find common ground for the sake of our child?*

Each situation is unique, but surely, we can address some of the most common challenges ahead, such as refraining from needless conflict, communicating more effectively, and considering co-parenting counseling.

Is there a new love on the horizon? We'll discuss how you can approach this touchy subject, too.

## HOW TO GET PAST CO-PARENTING OBSTACLES

Co-parenting difficulties cannot be solved in one step. Consistency, open communication, and the capacity to change course when necessary, will be required.

The following parts provide concrete suggestions for dealing with co-parenting difficulties:

### Refrain From Needless Conflict

Emotional reactions and disagreements between co-parents cause unnecessary problems. To prevent unnecessary conflicts, co-parents must be aware of when they are reacting emotionally rather than rationally. A rational and reasonable approach is sometimes preferable to an emotional one when resolving a disagreement.

By establishing and upholding co-parenting agreements, co-parents can also avert possible disputes.

They may provide guidelines for discipline, parenting, and lifestyle decisions.

This might involve deliberations and decisions regarding the following:

- Establishing routines for consistency, such as sleep or meals.
- Important activities and experiences, including finishing your schoolwork or participating in an activity.
- Cleanliness procedures or orderliness.
- Making financial allowances for purchases.
- How to proceed while making crucial choices for or concerning the child.
- How to organize visitors and transitions between houses.

As your child matures and their demands vary in lifestyle and finances, co-parenting arrangements may also alter, just as parents' lifestyles or financial situations. Even though there may still be certain fixed agreements between co-parents, these arrangements should allow for flexibility as families and lifestyles evolve.

### Use Active Listening Techniques

Communication is a key component of successful co-parenting.

Parents who actively listen to each other include:

- Give the speaker your undivided attention by stopping what you are doing.
- Make respectful eye contact and listen.
- Having empathy with the speaker while listening.
- Ensure you comprehend what they are saying, repeat what you have heard (this ensures that you learn the co-parents' perspectives without requiring you to agree with them).
- Limiting critique.
- Identifying the initial step in the solution-finding process.

Co-parents' communication and comprehension can be facilitated through active listening.

Other pointers for starting and keeping a conversation include:

- Setting a positive tone. Co-parents who may be going through emotional turmoil in their relationship might use a professional, courteous tone that conveys impartiality and respect.

- Instead of making demands or pronouncements, phrase and frame your requests as inquiries. This can entail saying, "Can we try XYZ?" Rather than "You should XYZ."
- Commit to keeping talks child-centered.
- Co-parents can also gain by being aware of and controlling their emotional triggers. This can entail being aware of your stress levels and learning to remain composed and in control when having a challenging conversation.

### Counseling

You could choose co-parenting counseling if you try several approaches to communication and negotiation and still can't come to an agreement. Counseling for co-parents might help them strike a balance between their duties. Parents seek healthy communication and conflict-resolution techniques in co-parenting treatment. Active participation in co-parenting treatment can aid parents in understanding and establishing limits for their co-parenting relationships.

## DATING AFTER A DIVORCE

Dating as a single parent is quite stressful. Your children may have strong ideas about your dating choices, making it challenging to find time to date. It's not unusual to date someone whose child doesn't like them, but should this be a deal-breaker in a relationship? No, not always.

Here are some actions you may take if your children

genuinely detest your partner, in addition to moving slowly and respecting their viewpoints.

### Where to Begin

The first step is determining why your child's resistance to your new partner bothers you. For example, suppose it bothers you that your child does not appear eager to get to know your new partner or establish a connection with them. In that case, you may need to be patient and compassionate toward your child.

They need room and time to adjust to your new relationship before they can fully embrace your new partner. While you and your partner can urge them to interact or get to know each other, it will be best for everyone to remain patient and go at your child's speed.

Continue to provide your child opportunities to interact, but accept their preferences and try not to press the issue.

If your child is exhibiting behavioral difficulties, addressing those concerns is often the first step you take to help your child improve their conduct. New behavioral problems are frequently a cry for support and attention. Make sure your children are your top priority. They might not be prepared to move on, even if you are eager to start dating again. Be patient with them as children discover how to make wiser decisions amid suffering and grief.

### Identify the True Problem

Some individuals think you should immediately quit a relationship if your child despises your new significant other. However, it might be optional to end the connection. If your child despises your partner or is just anxious about you dating, you need to figure out which is true. Reassure your child that they remain your top priority. You should also ask why your child disapproves of the person you're seeing, depending on their age.

While some children may have little trouble expressing their grievances, others may find it difficult. Regardless, showing compassion is essential by listening carefully and acknowledging their sentiments.

Here are some typical arguments for why children object to their parent's relationships, Your child might (Wolf, 2021):

- Feel in danger or isolated.
- Envy the time you two spend together.
- Consider your partner to be *trying to be too strict*.
- Try to stand up for or support the other parent.
- Feel ashamed of your love life.
- Need time to adjust or process the loss of their family.
- Discover a fault in your character that you were unaware of.
- Feel threatened by your new partner.
- Dislike the new partner's behavior or communication with them.

You must seriously consider the concerns raised by your child if they identify a character fault in your new partner, state that they feel uncomfortable, or signal that they believe your new partner to be a *nasty* person. Your child needs you to listen to them since looking at a new connection without being emotionally invested is hard.

It might be helpful to get the opinions of trusted loved ones about a matter. Close friends and family who have seen your new partner's interactions with your children might provide more nuanced criticism. Tell your child what they said, then inquire about their perception of the connection.

You should rethink dating this individual if your children and people closest to you notice a problem in the connection.

However, suppose your child is having trouble adjusting to the new person in their life and the changes that this person has brought for both of you. In that case, you should do everything possible to ease their transition.

This can entail putting your child's needs first and putting a temporary restriction on your time with your new partner. To give your child time to adjust, you may need to set limits on how much time your new partner may spend with them. Your child may eventually become comfortable spending time with your date as you introduce him or her to your dating partner.

### Discuss It With Your Child

Any successful partnership must have open communication as its foundation. Make sure you and your child have one-on-one time if your child hates your new partner and he or she is old enough to express their feelings.

Here are some suggestions to make your discussion flow more easily:

- **Make them feel comfortable asking you questions**: They may be curious about your motivations for starting a new relationship or the qualities you find attractive in this new partner. Or perhaps they're just curious as to why this newcomer smells so strongly of perfume. You can never tell what a child is thinking. Therefore, foster an atmosphere where children feel free to ask you any questions that come to mind.

- **Delegate some authority to your child**: A child's world might be upended when you start dating someone new since so much is out of their control. Give them control over when and how they see your new partner to help them adjust. Ask them if there is anything they would want to do as a group, such as go to the zoo, ride bikes, or see a movie. Invite them to participate in the decision-making process rather than just announcing it.
- **Give your child the power to impose boundaries**: To put it another way, if they express that they do not wish for your new partner to hug them or attend one of their soccer games, you should give some thought to granting their request. Trust takes time to develop. Therefore, even though you could be completely obsessed with your new love partner, your child might not feel the same way. Be patient, and let them explore their feelings for this new individual on their own time.
- **Describe the qualities of your new partner that you enjoy**: Let your children know the characteristics you look for in a partner and how your new one exhibits them. If you like, you may even give instances. Your child may adjust their viewpoint simply by hearing what you perceive.

- **Remind them of your love for them**: Give your child a big hug, a kiss, and reassurance that they will never lose their place in your heart despite the arrival of a new sibling. Also, resolve to meet often for time spent together. It makes sense that your child might start to dislike your new partner if you spend all of your time with them. Ensure that you are actively seeking a sense of balance.

### Make Your Child Feel Like They Belong

To help your child and your new partner get to know each other better in a non-threatening setting, try to create some chances for them to do so. For instance, try leaving the house and doing something enjoyable together to observe how the chance to have fun together affects their relationship.

Let them participate in decision-making to make your child more receptive to the experience.

When setting up dates, keep your child in mind as well. It may be easier on you in the short term to plan your dates around when your ex-partner is caring for the children. You won't pressure your children into a new relationship before they're ready.

Gradually, you can sometimes involve your new partner, such as during a family meal. But if you often leave them with a babysitter while you go on dates, they can grow to dislike this person before they ever get a chance to get to know them.

While you work through these issues, try to be understanding of your child. Children may find it challenging to deal with divorce even without having to deal with dating (Wolf, 2021).

## There Is Hope

Children usually despise the people on their parent's date, but it isn't any less complicated. The good news is that there are things that you can do to assist your children in adjusting to the person you are seeing. Spend time with them, listen to what they say, give them some control when you can, and validate their feelings.

However, the most crucial thing is to let them know that you still value and love them. Ensure them that you won't disappear and that this new individual won't take the place of their other parent. After some time has passed, your child may accept this newcomer and become friendlier. Go slowly and wait till that time comes. Below you'll find a dating checklist to help you decide whether this new love interest is worth your and your children's time.

## Dating Checklist

Create a list of the top five things that would cause you to back out of the relationship before it begins. Before you bring anyone else into the presence of your children.

Be sure you understand how they manage their own lives:

1. Are they secure in their financial situation?
2. Are they able to have a good time even when they don't have any alcohol or drugs in their system?
3. Do they enjoy spending time with children?
4. Are they effective communicators?
5. Are they patient?
6. How do they manage their anger?

7. Does he or she get along with their own family?
8. How do they handle their own money?
9. Do they have a clear understanding of the commitment you have made to your children?
10. Do they believe in not spanking children?

Take your time in determining whether this person has your and your children's best interests at heart. It's something you need to determine on your own; no one can make that decision for you, and no, you don't need anyone's permission to date or see someone. You are a grown adult, and you are allowed to love and spend your time with whomever you like. Just make sure they're the right fit for your children, too. As always, encourage healthy bonds, open communication, and sticking to your routine. If you and your new partner see each other every other Saturday to take the children for ice cream and a walk in the park, be sure to take them. Children need routine.

## MISTAKES IN PARENTAL DISCIPLINE

If only divorced parents could co-parent without any hitches, life would be much easier for everyone involved. There would be no deviation from the rules. The effects of the consequences would spread from one household to the next. And both of the child's parents would collaborate to head off any behavioral issues before they arose.

However, there is no denying that disagreement is most couples' primary cause of divorce. And there are several ways to raise children, which can lead to various approachcs to conflict. Even if you and your ex disagree on parenting, you can teach your child how to handle their behavior. When going through a divorce, many parents make the mistake of losing sight of the most effective way to discipline their children.

And unfortunately, even well-meaning parents frequently fall victim to the following blunders (Morin, 2016):

1. **Behaving Deceptively**

Occasionally, a parent may say, "He never misbehaves while he's at my place." I don't know what causes him to misbehave at your place. When your child is in your care, however, insisting that he or she behaves like a flawless angel will not do anybody any favors.

Likewise, avoid working with your child to exaggerate his positive traits. Sometimes, parents will say things to their children like, "We won't tell Dad that you were in trouble in the classroom, all right?" A harmful message is sent when there is an agreement to keep secrets regarding his actions.

Openly discuss with your ex the behavior you are observing and the corrective measures you are taking. Open communication may be the first step in finding a solution to an issue, even though the house rules and penalties for breaking those rules can differ from household to household.

To address a problem constructively, you must first determine its frequency and the context in which it manifests before you can do anything else.

Speak out and be truthful about what's happening to determine whether a certain behavior is a one-time or recurring problem.

## 2. Feeling Bad for Your Child

When a couple separates, it's not uncommon for the parents to view their child as the victim of the separation. As a result, their discipline becomes more lenient.

Saying things like, "Well, they've already gone through so much. I don't want to remove their video games from them," or "She is simply misbehaving because she's distressed from the divorce. I don't want to punish her any further;" that is not a good idea!

Your child will develop a victim mentality if you teach them that they are a "product of divorce" by introducing such phrases. Recognize and validate their emotions. Discuss their difficulties, but remind them that difficulties should not be used as a reason or, rather, an excuse for poor behavior.

You can help your child by correcting their actions, but not their feelings. Allow them to be angry, scared, or sad. Aside from giving them space to grieve, teach them healthy coping mechanisms for dealing with complicated feelings.

Your child could require expert assistance if they are having difficulty adjusting. Consult your child's physician if you notice any significant behavioral or mood changes that last more than a few weeks.

But keep in mind that divorce does not permanently harm children. Divorce may even be a relief if you are in a high-conflict relationship. There are situations when a child's behavior will improve after their parents are separated.

## 3. Having Inconsistent Rules

The rules and the consequences for breaking them still need

to be communicated to the children. In actuality, maintaining a regular discipline routine will aid your child in feeling safe and comfortable. At the same time, he adjusts to new and sometimes stressful circumstances.

However, maintaining consistency becomes more difficult after a divorce. You need to remember to ask yourself whether or not you revoked his permission to play video games within five minutes of his leaving to go to his other parent's place. If that's the case, can you wait till he returns to impose the consequence?

Naturally, you'll also feel the effects of the strain caused by your separation and divorce. It may be more challenging to maintain a routine and apply clear repercussions when you are a single parent because of your additional duties.

4. **Differences in Discipline**

After a divorce, parenting techniques may become more apparent, such as imposing consequences and establishing household norms and standards. A 50/50 split of the children between the parents might make this situation worse.

Setting two different standards for behavior and regulations at home might lead to inconsistency and confusion in a child's life. Parents who differ on the guidelines may impose different degrees of ongoing disciplinary measures. When a child switches to the other parent's home for a week of custody after breaking a rule in one household and receiving a week of being grounded, the other parent is not required to continue the discipline.

This might lead to the first parent being seen as uncaring and disrespectful. For the child, who might find it challenging to grasp limits, consistency, and rules, this can lead to discrepancies.

5. **Communication Difficulties**

Some people may have decided to get divorced or separated amicably. There can be some negative emotions for others. To co-parent successfully, however, communication must continue until the child is at least 18 years old.

Co-parents frequently encounter the following communication difficulties:

- Communication difficulties are caused by negative emotions like wrath, hostility, resentment, or hate.
- Regularly dissenting from the other parent's parenting strategies or decisions in life.
- The act of one co-parent lying to the child or speaking negatively about the other co-parent in front of the child.
- One co-parent fails to communicate with the other, fails to show up for scheduled appointments, or neglects the child.
- Co-parents don't appreciate or understand each other.

Children may need clarification on various parenting philosophies and inconsistent encouragement and messages. Screen time, for instance, can be restricted in one home but supported and promoted in another. Or, one house may have a more relaxed attitude about diet than the other. Parents may differ on important issues affecting their child's development, leading to contradictory lifestyles and decisions in the child's life between the two homes.

6. **Financial Inequality Amongst Households**

The following are some of the most common problems with money and money inequality:

- One parent's lack of financial support. As children get older, their financial demands vary, and they could incur new costs not previously covered by child support arrangements.
- Child support arrangements could need to be revised if there are shifts in the co-parents' respective wages or in the amount of time spent with the child(ren).
- Co-parents may have financial disparities because one parent chooses to give their children more expensive resources (such as clothing, things, or experiences) than the other parent can afford.
- Co-parenting relationships can become strained and challenging due to financial dynamics that are frequently difficult to discuss or deal with. These issues have a direct influence on the child's wellness.

7. **Refusing to Collaborate as a Team**

Parents frequently refuse to compromise while working together to find solutions to problems. It is not helpful to skip a school gathering because you think your ex will hold you responsible for anything or to refuse to see a therapist because you didn't choose that person.

Your willingness to work with your ex and any professionals tackling behavioral difficulties will be much appreciated. Be open to suggestions, and at the very least, be prepared to hear criticism.

Listening is the first step, even if you disagree with your partner's assessment of the child's behavior or overlook the same issues. Showing you're willing to listen to the problems is the first step in finding a solution.

Now that we've discussed how to conquer the challenges that might arise during co-parenting, the final chapter will help restore a sense of calm and balance to this journey.

# CHAPTER 8: FINDING BALANCE

The relationship between a parent and a child helps the child grow in all aspects of their being, including their body, emotions, and relationships with others. It is a special connection that may be enjoyed and fostered by every child and parent. This bond forms the basis for the child's personality, the decisions they will make throughout life, and general behavior.

Here we'll look at how you can cultivate positive parenting relationships and discuss what this journey can teach your child.

## HAVE A POSITIVE RELATIONSHIP WITH YOUR CHILD

There is no "one size fits all" approach to raising children; parents must evolve and adapt with their children.

However, adopting some easy positive parenting guidelines can improve your connection to your child (*Parent-Child Relationship—Why It's Important*, 2018):

1. **Interactions Full of Love and Warmth**

Approach each encounter with your child as a chance to strengthen your bond with them. Make an effort to convey warmth via your expressions by smiling, making eye contact, and encouraging engagement.

## 2. **Boundaries, Rules, and Consequences**

The development of children requires structure and direction. Make sure your children know your expectations for them by explaining them in clear terms.

Boundaries serve as a bridge between various viewpoints and a starting point for honest conversation. When communicating their values to their co-parent to improve their ability to cooperate for the benefit of their children, one parent might set boundaries with that person. The other parent could share the same values as you, like encouraging open communication, but their definitions might differ. It doesn't make one viewpoint superior to the other. Rather, it involves bargaining to find a solution that benefits all sides.

In a few rare circumstances, a hard NO will be justified. A parent or child may undergo emotional, psychological, sexual, drug, or physical abuse at the hands of another person.

Parents frequently feel they have the last word in their home, which is another typical belief. While this is true, children also have expectations of what their parents should do to earn their respect and cooperation. When parents have a higher level of respect for their children, there will be more love and comprehension in the home.

*How do children's boundaries appear when their parents are divorced?*

The following are some boundaries for children who need to be with their divorced parents:

### 1. **Avoid Acting as a Parent's Emotional Support System**

Being a parent on your own is challenging, especially if you don't have much help from others. You could have had to pack up your entire life and relocate to a different place due to the divorce if it left you with few friends, a resentful family, or neither. While going through a divorce may be extremely taxing, expecting your children to support you emotionally may be asking too much of them.

Children are frequently too young to comprehend the nuances of divorce or the factors that ultimately cause the couple to split up. Usually, when their parents are upset, the children will see it and ask why their parents cry more often than they laugh. If you confide in your child to support you emotionally, they may even believe the divorce is their fault.

Give your child the childhood you would like them to have so they may flourish and get used to their new way of life.

### 2. **Not to Take Care of Siblings All the Time**

You might want to get out and start engaging in new social contacts as you transition from being in a partnership to being single. However, suppose you expect your eldest child to babysit regularly throughout your parenting time, just as you may go out on dates. In that case, you may be pushing your oldest child's limitations for how much time they want to spend with their family. When children are pushed to become adults before they are ready, they might become "parentified." This indicates that the child assumes parental responsibilities much too early in life before they are ready to handle them.

Possible long-term implications of being parentified include failing to develop emotionally, regressing as they grow older, worrying excessively that the family will break apart if they don't take on the burden, and seeking out caregivers in romantic relationships as adults. This may result in an endless cycle of unsatisfying relationships.

### 3. Not to Be Forced Into Having Relationships With Stepparents

Children mustn't be pushed into a parent-like connection with their stepparents just because they spend time with them at both houses. By engaging in straightforward conversations where they may develop friendship and trust, children will innately choose to respect their stepparent's relationship.

Even though stepparents may be fantastic additional parents for children, a child will build a bond with a stepparent when it seems right to them. Children seek safety and security before connecting with anyone other than their biological parents since they are still figuring out connections and who is looking out for them.

Suppose the stepparent's behavior isn't nurturing to the child. In that case, the youngster may withdraw from the stepparent for fear of being criticized or told what to do. Children appreciate people who respect their boundaries, pay attention to their worries and anxieties, comprehend how they feel, and assist them by being supportive and encouraging.

Developing a strong bond with the stepparents and children will be simpler if they have a positive dynamic.

## Be Patient and Understanding With Your Child

Acknowledge the sensations your child is experiencing, demonstrate that you understand them, and tell them that you will assist them whenever they experience difficulty.

## How to Improve the Parent-Child Relationship

Building a strong relationship of trust and respect between a parent and child requires establishing a connection with the youngster.

These techniques can help you bond with your children:

- **Share how much you care for them**: You should make it clear to your children every day that you love them, regardless of how old they are. Even on challenging days, make it clear to your child that even if you are disappointed in their behavior, they are always loved no matter what. A relationship may be significantly strengthened by saying, "I love you."
- **Have some fun together**: Children's growth is greatly aided by their time spent playing. Play is an important vehicle for developing a wide range of competencies in young children. It may improve children's language abilities, emotions, creativity, and social skills, in addition to being enjoyable and fostering closer relationships between you and your child.
- **Be available**: Put aside time each day to sit down and have an uninterrupted conversation with your child; even ten minutes may significantly impact the

development of healthy communication routines. Put away the gadgets and turn off the television to enjoy quality time with your loved ones.

- **Eat together**: When a family sits down to a meal together, it creates an atmosphere conducive to discourse. Encourage everyone to put down their devices and just enjoy one another's company instead.
- **Pay attention and show empathy**: Listening is the foundation of connection. You should perceive things from the point of view of your child and cultivate mutual respect.
- **Spend time with them on a one-on-one basis**: It's essential to treat each of your children individually, even if you have many children. Spending focused, one-on-one time with your child may fortify your relationship with them, boost their sense of self-worth, and convey that their contributions are appreciated.

## PRACTICE POSITIVE SHARED PARENTING

It is unreasonable to assume that your parenting approach will not be altered because you are divorcing or no longer living together. Still, it's in everyone's best interest to take an open and honest look at your parenting every once in a while.

Although children do not demand perfection from you, they do demand fairness. If your parenting approach is veering into potentially harmful terrain, be honest with yourself and your children about the error.

It is feasible to improve your parenting approach with a few little changes. Co-parenting might sometimes be challenging, but you should always keep things civil and cooperative. Positive parenting techniques can assist you both in maintaining this focus.

Positive parenting is the ongoing interaction between parents and their children. It entails loving, teaching, taking the lead, communicating, and consistently and unconditionally meeting their child's needs (Lonczak, 2019).

## Positive Approaches to Parenting

Positive parenting research always returns to the idea that a parenting style that is both warm and firm is associated with a broader range of successful outcomes for children and adolescents. This method of parenting is referred to as "authoritative." It is seen as a style that strikes a healthy balance between parental characteristics: aggressive but not invasive; demanding yet responsive; helpful in discipline; and not punishing (Lonczak, 2019).

A developing parenting style is thought to foster successful child outcomes in addition to an authoritarian parenting style.

Affection, by making warm and encouraging gestures toward the child; responsiveness, by observing the child's signs; encouragement, by fostering the child's talents and interests;

and instruction, through the use of play and discussion to foster the child's cognitive development, are all components of the positive parenting approach known as developmental parenting (Lonczak, 2019).

Both developmental parenting and authoritative parenting are examples of effective parenting styles, and they have several characteristics that are similar to one another.

In a nutshell, loving, supportive, firm, consistent, and active parents contribute to a child's positive growth and development of the inner spirit. These parents don't just tell their children what they expect of them; they also provide a good example for them to follow.

## An Examination of Positive Discipline

Because it should be given in a way that is both tough and caring at the same time, positive discipline calls to mind authoritative parenting once again. Positive discipline is not punitive; it is never violent, angry, or critical.

Positive discipline has five requirements (Lonczak, 2019):

- It is firm yet also compassionate.
- Helps a child feel like they belong and gives them a sense of purpose.
- Maintains its effectiveness over time.
- Teaches important social and practical skills.

Encourages children to see themselves as strong and independent individuals.

The main features of positive discipline are that it is non-violent, polite, and based on developmental principles. It teaches children to respect themselves, empathize with others, and be self-sufficient.

Teaching children that even the tiniest, most helpless, and most vulnerable person deserves respect is a lesson our world needs to learn and one that can be imparted to them by valuing them.

The next logical question is, "Exactly what does positive discipline involve?" since we know that punishment is never used.

## Practical Positive Parenting

As parents, we will inevitably mess up and lose our tempers. That gives us a perfect chance to make amends with our children and demonstrate how we can bounce back after making mistakes.

Positive parenting involves five steps (McCready, 2021):

### 1. Dedicate Some Time to Talking to Each Other

By far, the most effective thing you can do to assist your children in developing self-confidence through healthy relationships is to spend regular bonding time with them and model good conduct for them.

Children naturally desire loving attention and emotional ties with other people. Parents are left to cope with power struggles, whining, and meltdowns from their children when they don't get it, as their children start looking for it in unhealthy ways. Enjoying your small moments of connection with your child can contribute to developing a deeper and more significant relationship.

### 2. Establish Ground Rules for "When-Then" Situations

A fundamental component of effective parenting is communicating openly and unambiguously about one's goals and objectives. To encourage good behavior during the periods of the day that are the most trying for you and your child, the "when-then" strategy is one that I recommend implementing.

Explain to your child that after the unpleasant part of a task they don't want to complete is over, the more fun parts may begin. If they have time until the bus arrives, they can play outdoors or use their iPad after cleaning their teeth, dressing, and eating breakfast.

If you continue this habit, your children will rapidly learn to complete the steps independently without your help. No nagging is necessary.

### 3. Decide Against Rewards

Children who are praised and rewarded frequently are likely to lose interest in the specific behavior for which they are praised and rewarded. This holds regardless of whether the activity being praised and rewarded is playing ball with a sibling or practicing an instrument. They'll start caring more about the rewards, which means you might have to keep giving them out to keep them behaving the same.

The use of encouragement is a more effective method for highlighting the best in our children. However, one should steer clear of terms that reference their nature or demeanor, such as "You're so clever!"

Encourage the particular action in its place. For instance, if your child expresses care for someone who appears sad, praise them for their good behavior by saying, "That was sweet of you to ask if your sister is okay." Stress how much the other individual could have valued their thoughtful action.

### 4. Show Them the Relevant Consequences

When a youngster starts acting out, using natural consequences, or showing how things might unfold can transform poor decisions into learning opportunities for the child.

When your children refuse to wear rubber boots on a cold and rainy morning, explain the direct outcome: their socks will be damp, and their feet will become uncomfortably wet. In this way, it will make the consequence feel less like punishment because the child will have some control over it.

This gives your child the freedom to decide whether or not they want to wear boots so that they can figure out the best choice for themselves.

### 5. Concentrate on the Things Under Your Control

Your child may not always behave as you expect them to, but you have control over how you react to their actions. This frame of mind can empower children to take on chores that, usually, you would have to remind them about, such as cleaning up their lunch boxes.

For example, "I'll gladly prepare your school lunch if you just empty and clean up your lunchbox beforehand." Then, assist them in locating means by which they may remember their obligation and carry it out, such as a visual reminder in the form of a note on the fridge. Your child will learn a lot about responsibility and independence by making his or her lunch.

Building respectful relationships based on clear expectations is the key to positive parenting. It is far more probable that children will act correctly and grow up to be resilient, confident, kind, and responsible if they have a good relationship with their parents. This section has offered many valuable suggestions for positive discipline that may be used in various challenging parenting circumstances. A practical method of discipline that fosters loving connections between parents and children while also generating productive, polite, and happy children is known as "positive discipline."

We, as parents, can confidently take on our roles as educators, leaders, and mentors because of the abundance of helpful parenting solutions and tools. And in the end, we will develop close, lifelong bonds with our children by constantly employing positive parenting techniques.

## WHAT WILL DIVORCE TEACH MY CHILD?

It's true that parents strive hard to educate their children about right and wrong. Still, it's also true that children learn from their surroundings even when adults aren't trying to teach them anything. Children learn much more by seeing what we do than by listening to what we have to say, regardless of how hard we try to communicate with them. When a couple breaks up or gets divorced, the children will have a front-row seat to see how their parents deal with complicated feelings and arguments. They will only hold it against you if you nail every landing. Still, they will get significant insight from observing how you generally work through the difficulties associated with co-parenting.

When planning your child's separation education, keep these three C's in mind to give them the best possible footing for handling future conflicts.

## Communication

Almost no parent gets a divorce or separates without having at least some fights. When a significant relationship ends, people almost always feel strong emotions. No one expects parents to conceal their emotional reactions totally; nevertheless, when strong sentiments cause seemingly endless conflict or unpleasant disagreements, it's essential to consider how you're teaching your child to treat others while they're in the thick of a disagreement.

You probably don't want your child to pick up on your snide remarks, silence, stonewalling, or refusal to compromise, so try to avoid doing these things yourself as much as possible. When you make a mistake, you must move on and make things right. Your child will learn how to recover from short-term setbacks and take criticism of their actions in stride. Nobody can claim to be flawless. You'll have the opportunity to show people early and frequently that being flawed doesn't have to be a recipe for ongoing conflict.

If your family has a history of conflict due to poor communication, modeling flexibility by identifying and eliminating the causes is one way to instill it in your children. You and your co-parent may not be able to talk to each other like you did before you split up. If you and your co-parent change how you talk to each other and keep up with positive parenting, you will show your child that there is never one way to solve a problem.

## Coping

When things are hard, it's easy to forget about taking care of yourself. Poor coping skills can show up in many ways, like bad eating habits, being too sensitive, or being too tired to do much of anything. These problems can last longer and affect how a child handles similar stresses in adulthood. Separation can bring up new, stressful feelings that can make you feel tired, unmotivated, and unable to deal with stress healthily. Still, showing your child how to deal with problems in a healthy way is essential because those are the same skills they'll use as adults.

It's not wrong to reward yourself with a sweet treat once in a while if you're feeling down, but how can you know if your coping mechanisms have gone too far? If the ways you relax start to lead to bad or unhealthy habits, it's time to rethink how you deal with stress in your everyday life. Self-care may be done in many straightforward ways. Still, if your stress or suffering is too great for you to handle, it might be time to get professional assistance. Seeing a therapist help you through these problems will show your child that it takes courage to ask for help when needed. Teaching children that grit doesn't need isolation and that community can serve as a tremendous source of comfort may be as simple as modeling the behavior of asking for help when we need it.

## Compassion

Putting your needs aside when going through a divorce or separation can be challenging. With so many different things happening daily, it's easy to give in to the temptation to take advantage of every chance to get what you want. Most of the time, this urge can lead to small things that make it hard to compromise. When you let this way of thinking take control of your thoughts, it is easy to ignore requests made by your co-parent, even if those demands are harmless or acceptable.

Countering this tendency by prioritizing your child's needs over your own (even if it means doing a favor for your co-parent) may teach your child valuable lessons in empathy and understanding. If you made decisions based on what was in the child's best interests, even if it meant giving in to the other parent, they would grow up understanding how much you cared about them. By doing so, you will demonstrate to them that selflessness is possible even in the face of adversity.

Your children will look to you as a role model for their lives, studying how you handle difficult situations, interact with people, and resolve disagreements. With the uncertainty that comes with separation, your children will watch you even more closely during this time. Give your children the tools necessary to handle similar circumstances long into adulthood by being conscious of the lessons your actions will teach them about conflict and working hard to be a positive example for them.

### Pledge of Co-parenting

This is your pledge to help you commit to being the best parent you can be:

- I've decided to stop dwelling on the past and instead put my energy towards planning for the future. I will not put our children in circumstances over which they have no control.

- I will not expect the children to cope with adult concerns, but I will listen intently to every family member. First, comprehend them and then make them feel understood.
- I will speak to the other parent directly about significant concerns like money, time-sharing, and scheduling adjustments.
- I will not argue with the other parent in the presence of the children.
- I will acknowledge that we have different points of view and suggest setting up a meeting where we can concentrate on finding a solution.
- I will let all of our friends and family members know. In particular, our grandparents know that they should support the co-parenting duties we have taken on and that any talk involving the children should be positive and supportive.
- I will set an example for self-care by treating myself to four wonderful things each week to make me feel better and become a better parent.
- As a parent, I pledge to use strategies to correct my child's behavior that encourages them to think critically about the world around them, find constructive solutions to problems, and use fair, appropriate, empathetic, and educational consequences.
- Before introducing anyone to our children, we agree to go through the dating checklist.
- We are willing to agree to settle contentious matters with a knowledgeable third party who can point us on the most beneficial path for our

children while allowing us to sidestep the expense of legal action.

Date: __________Co-Parent: __________

It is possible, however challenging, for parents to gracefully navigate such a trying situation with their children. You may improve your ability to be a good co-parent by cultivating healthy boundaries, compassion, open communication, and consistency in your interactions. The good news? It can work without you being close to your ex-partner.

# CONCLUSION: A LAST LETTER TO YOU

Through the practice known as "co-parenting," both biological parents take on a shared role in the care and upbringing of their child. You will be doing your child a favor by making every attempt to co-parent with the other parent of your child effectively. This is a gift you can give your child. Co-parenting is essential for your child's health, even though it isn't always a simple task.

This book has guided readers on how to successfully put co-parenting into reality by exploring your thoughts on the process, how your child could feel the divorce, and how you might handle problem behavioral and acute emotional issues—providing parenting ideas that transform one's viewpoint and solutions for specific problems that may arise. This comprehensive guide will help you raise your children in a secure, loving, and accepting atmosphere while preparing them for a life of self-regulation, independence, and resilience.

When both parents agree to do what is best for their child, they will be better able to work together for the benefit of their child. Each parent acknowledges the other parent's right to engage in parenting. They come to an understanding with one another over specific, fundamental parenting guidelines. The parents can let go of their hostility toward one another and commit to co-parenting their child warmly and caringly.

Remind yourself that your child loves this other person and that the end you want for your child is for them to have both of you in their life, even if it means working through some disagreements. You and your child's other parent are still considered co-parents, even though there is no longer any romantic involvement between you. Children fare best when raised by two loving, harmonious parents who can put their differences aside for the sake of their child. Your child will value the time and effort you put into providing a loving and supportive environment for him or her by working together with the other parent in a cooperative manner.

You are now aware of how to establish boundaries, engage in good parenting, and practice tactics that will assist your child in navigating their own space and time. The only thing left to do is put this new information into practice; if you get lost along the way, come back to this book for help, and keep in mind that you, too, are only human.

You can reclaim control of your life and look forward with excitement to this new adventure. This is your opportunity to build the kind of family life and environment you've always dreamed of having.

You still want to take the children to Disneyland for a vacation. Have fun with that vacation! Make brand-new memories, and value the time you spend together.

Give your children the most excellent possible upbringing while also instilling in them the positive parenting ideals that will equip them to deal with any challenges that life may throw at them.

You've got this from one co-parent to another.

## THANK YOU

As an author, I would be grateful if you could take a moment to leave a review of the book. Reviews not only provide valuable feedback for me as an author, but they also help other readers decide whether to read the book.

Reviews can make a huge difference in the success of a book. They can help the book reach a wider audience, gain more exposure, and ultimately, enable me to continue writing and publishing more books.

I'd be very grateful if you would consider leaving a review on Amazon. It only takes a few minutes, but it can have a lasting impact.

Thank you once again for your support, and I hope you enjoy reading more books in the future.

# AUTHOR

Let me introduce myself. My name is Willem Cunningham, and I'll be your guide as you navigate the tricky terrain of co-parenting after a divorce.

Outdoor activities, like excursions to the beach, long walks in the city along the river, and early morning visits to nature parks, are some of my favorite ways to spend time with my two daughters, ages 7 and 9. In addition to that, I find regular exercise and cooking up a storm in the kitchen to be quite relaxing.

I place a lot of importance on improving myself, and I do so daily. As much as I can, I instill in my daughters a love of learning and a positive outlook on life.

Reading and writing have always been activities I've taken great pleasure in, and I am doing my best to pass this on to my girls.

I'm now going through the co-parenting process, as are many others worldwide, so I choose to specialize in this subject. When parents separate, it will always be difficult for both of them, but it will be especially difficult for the parent who has to leave home and start over, whether that person is the mother or the father.

It is already challenging enough to be a parent in this day and age when the children we are raising are more easily distracted than ever before. Our abilities as parents are always being tested, regardless of whether we're talking about the television, cell phones, or social media. When you consider the reality that some children are raised in two different houses, the daily task becomes enormous. This book is written from the heart and based on the lessons I've learned as time passes.

I'm writing this book to offer a practical and empathetic perspective on parenting after divorce. Even the most challenging talks with children and ex-partners may be handled easily because of the user-friendly structure, which blends bulleted lists with helpful tips, exercises, and sample dialogues. Most essential, this book gives divorced parents the tools they need to be the greatest co-parents they can be: capable, loving, present, and responsible individuals who lead by example.

Being a father after a divorce has been the most challenging and testing adventure ever. It has been replete with many unexpected rewards and challenges that I could never have anticipated. As I write this book, I hope to pave an enlightening way forward not only for you as a reader and a fellow co-parent but also for myself. one that will push me to be more, show me what I'm already doing well, give me hope and confidence that I can still develop into the greatest possible parent that I can be for my two beautiful children, and challenge me to be more than I currently am.

I hope you've found *A Guide to Parenting Emotionally Strong Children* helpful in improving your co-parenting journey for the benefit of your children. As an independent author, your feedback is invaluable as I strive to improve and grow with each book I write. This book may serve as a lighthouse for anyone navigating the uncertain waters of parenthood during and after divorce, providing guidance and support to help you and your children navigate this difficult transition with strength and resilience.

# BIBLIOGRAPHY

Ahrons, C. R. (2007, April). *Family Ties After Divorce: Long-Term Implications for Children.* Research Gate. https://www.researchgate.net/publication/6431031_Family_Ties_After_Divorce_Long-Term_Implications_for_Children

*Behavioral Issues in Children After Divorce.* (2023). Our Family Wizard. https://www.ourfamilywizard.com/blog/behavioral-issues-children-after-divorce#:~:text=It%20is%20not%20abnormal%20for,events%20happening%20in%20their%20life

Bieber, C. (2022, December 15). *Divorce With Kids: Everything You Need To Know.* Forbes. https://www.forbes.com/advisor/legal/divorce/divorce-with-kids/

Brady, G. (2013, December 19). *Children's Emotional Needs During Divorce and Beyond.* Finding Common Ground. https://www.findingcommonground.-com/childrens-emotional-needs-during-divorce-and-beyond-by-paul-wanio-phd-lmft/

Broadwell, L. (2022). *Effects of Divorce on Children: An Age-by-Age Guide.* Parents. https://www.parents.com/parenting/divorce/coping/age-by-age-guide-to-what-children-understand-about-divorce/

Buie, E. (2021, March 16). *7 Behaviors Parents Should Look Out for in Children During Divorce.* Elise Buie Family Law. https://elisebuiefamilylaw.com/7-behaviors-parents-should-look-out-for-in-children-during-divorce/

Chasse, B. M. (2021, March). *The Art of Effective Co-Parenting.* Good Therapy. https://www.goodtherapy.org/blog/Art-of-Effective-Coparenting

*Child Psychology and Mental Health.* (2022, February). Child Development Institute. https://childdevelopmentinfo.com/child-psychology/

*Co-Parenting Challenges and Solutions.* (2021, June 8). Blake and Detchemendy Law Firm. https://www.augustafamilylawyer.com/challenges-of-co-parenting-and-how-to-overcome-them/

*Co-Parenting Series: Developmentally Appropriate Parenting Plans.* (2017, March). Oklahoma State University. https://extension.okstate.edu/fact-sheets/co-parenting-series-developmentally-appropriate-parenting-plans.html#:~:text=2021-,3.%20Children%E2%80%99s%20needs%20and%20lifestyles%20at%20each%20age%20level.,visit%20prospective%20colleges%2C%20and%20attend%20a%20child%E2%80%99s%20ball%20games%20and%20performances.,Write%20plans%20for%20level.,visit%20prospective%20colleges%2C%20and%20attend%20a%20child%E2%80%99s%20ball%20games%20and%20performances.,-Write%20plans%20for

*Coping With Separation And Divorce.* (2023). Mental Health America. https://www.mhanational.org/separation-and-divorce

Dixon, M. (2017, March 7). *Changes in the Parent-Child Relationship After Divorce.* Good Therapy. https://www.goodtherapy.org/blog/changes-in-parent-child-relationship-after-divorce-0307175

Engler, B. (2022, September 2). *Teaching Your Child to Deal with Conflict.* Connections Academy. https://www.connectionsacademy.com/support/resources/article/building-conflict-resolution-skills-in-children/

Fisher, D. (2019, March 18). *Children of divorce: the role of self-esteem in recovering from trauma.* Child and Family Blog. https://childandfamilyblog.com/children-of-divorce-self-esteem/

*Has Divorce Changed Your Parenting Style?* (2023). Our Family Wizard. https://www.ourfamilywizard.com/blog/has-divorce-changed-your-parenting-style

*Helping Children Cope with Divorce.* (2020). One Tough Job. https://onetoughjob.org/articles/helping-children-cope-with-divorce

*How to be a Better Parent: 10 Self-Reflection Questions.* (2020, May 19). The Rooted Family. https://www.therootedfamily.com/blog/how-to-be-a-better-parent

*How To Debunk Your Child's Post-Divorce Fears.* (2023). Our Family Wizard. https://www.ourfamilywizard.com/blog/how-debunk-your-childs-post-divorce-fears

*How to Raise a Socially Intelligent Child.* (2022). Aha Parenting. https://www.ahaparenting.com/guide/socially-intelligent

Isbill, J. (2020, November 26). *Extra Pressure of Divorced and Separated Parents with Children.* Medium. https://medium.com/age-of-empathy/divorced-and-separated-parents-with-children-feel-extra-pressured-95e0ba930da8

Jillian, & Jan. (2021, June 23). *How To Help Your Children of Divorce Set Boundaries.* Mediation & Coaching. https://www.divorcefamilymediations.-com/post/how-to-help-your-children-of-divorce-set-boundaries

Lonczak, H. S. (2019, May 8). *What is Positive Parenting? 33 Examples and Benefits.* Positive Psychology. https://positivepsychology.com/positive-parenting/

Maria. (2022, June 26). *24 Shadow Work Journal Prompts to Heal and Grow.* Aimlief. https://aimlief.com/shadow-work-journal-prompts/

Martelo, C. (2022, November 18). *What is positive parenting self-reflection?* Huckleberry. https://huckleberrycare.com/blog/what-is-positive-parenting-self-reflection

McCready, A. (2021, December 4). *Here's what makes "positive parenting" different*

—*and why experts say it's one of the best parenting styles.* CNBC. https://www.cnbc.com/2021/12/04/why-psychologists-say-positive-parenting-is-the-best-style-for-raising-confident-successful-kids.html

McGhee, C. (2013, August 29). *Adjustment Factors for Children of Divorce.* Divorce and Children. https://divorceandchildren.com/adjustment-factors-children-and-divorce/

Miller, W. (2020, June 20). *8 Things to Reflect on After Divorce.* Medium. https://wendymillermeditation.medium.com/8-things-to-reflect-on-after-divorce-73fbcee1fe07

Morin, A. (2015). *How to Raise Mentally Strong Kids.* Verywell Family. https://www.verywellfamily.com/tips-for-raising-mentally-strong-kids-1095020

Morin, A. (2016). *The Biggest Discipline Mistakes Divorced Parents Tend to Make.* Verywell Family. https://www.verywellfamily.com/parenting-mistakes-after-divorce-4084363

Morin, A. (2020). *Prevent Behavior Problems by Teaching Your Child About Feelings.* Verywell Family. https://www.verywellfamily.com/how-to-teach-kids-about-feelings-1095012

*Parent-Child Relationship—Why it's Important. (*2018, October 25). Parenting NI. https://www.parentingni.org/blog/parent-child-relationship-why-its-important/#:~:text=The%20Parent%2DChild%20Relationship%20is,life%20choices%20and%20overall%20behaviour

Perkel, J. (2022). *The Impact of Divorce on Children.* Psychology Today. https://www.psychologytoday.com/us/blog/21st-century-childhood/202208/the-impact-divorce-children

*Positive Principles of Co-Parenting.* (2021, December 14). Newport Divorce Attorney. https://www.newportdivorceattorney.com/positive-principles-of-co-parenting/#:~:text=There%20are%20four%20main%20principles,with%20both%20of%20their%20parents

*Restructuring Your Family After Divorce.* (2022). Our Family Wizard. https://www.ourfamilywizard.com/blog/restructuring-your-family-after-divorce

Schwartz, B. (2022). *The Effects of Divorce on Children & How to Help them Cope.* Choosing Therapy. https://www.choosingtherapy.com/divorce-and-children/

Sherrell, Z. (2022, March 30). *What to know about co-parenting.* Medical News Today.https://www.medicalnewstoday.com/articles/co-parenting#challenges

*Six Ways To Improve How You Navigate Change.* (2022, July 5). Individual, Relationship, Couples & Marriage Therapy. https://ftajax.com/improve-how-you-navigate-change/

Smith, K. (2022, August 12). *Tips to Cope With the Stress of a Divorce.* Psych Central.https://psychcentral.com/stress/reduce-the-stress-of-a-divorce#recap

Stone, E. (2022, June 16). *5 Emotional Self-Regulation Skills for Kids.* Mightier. https://www.mightier.com/resources/5-emotional-self-regulation-skills-for-kids/

*Stress Symptoms, Signs, and Causes.* (2013). Help Guide. https://www.helpguide.org/articles/stress/stress-symptoms-signs-and-causes.htm

*Stress: Signs, Symptoms, Management & Prevention.* (2021). Cleveland Clinic. https://my.clevelandclinic.org/health/articles/11874-stress

*Ten ways to nurture your child's self-concept.* (2023). Calm 4 kids. https://calm4kids.org/10-ways-to-nurture-your-childs-self-concept/

Tiret, H. B. (2012, August 3). *Ten tips for successful co-parenting.* MSU Extension. https://www.canr.msu.edu/news/ten_tips_for_successful_co-parenting

Trigueros, R., Sanchez-Sanchez, E., Mercader, I., Aguilar-Parra, J. M., López-Liria, R., Morales-Gázquez, M. J., Fernández-Campoy, J. M., & Rocamora, P. (2020). *Relationship between Emotional Intelligence, Social Skills and Peer Harassment. A Study with High School Students.* International Journal of Environmental Research and Public Health, *17*(12), 4208. https://doi.org/10.3390/ijerph17124208

Wake Forest University. (2017, January 31). *Counseling Children Through Divorce.* WFU Online Counseling. https://counseling.online.wfu.edu/blog/counseling-children-through-divorce/#:~:text=School%20counselors%20are%20often%20a,misbehavior%20resulting%20from%20emotional%20issues.&text=In%20some%20cases%2C%20school%20counselors,privacy%2C%20 and%20well%2Dbeing

Williams, C. (2021). *Five Surprisingly Favorable Effects of Divorce on Children.* Onward App. https://www.onwardapp.com/blog/effects-of-divorce-on-children

Wolf, J. (2021). *Are Your Kids Ready for You to Start Dating Again?* Verywell Family. https://www.verywellfamily.com/when-your-kids-hate-who-youre-dating-2997328

Young. (2019, December 3). *How to Cope with Divorce Stress.* Griffith Young & Lass. https://www.gylfamilylawfirm.com/blog/2019/december/how-to-cope-with-divorce-stress-by-family-attorn/

## IMAGE REFERENCES

Bauso, O. (2019). *Man in Pink Shirt Lifting up Girl* [Image]. Unsplash. https://unsplash.com/photos/6oRBgkX9UMI

Borba, J. (2019a). *Woman Holding Baby Up* [Image]. Unsplash. https://unsplash.com/photos/oHB7VKdpHQM

Borba, J. (2019b). *Woman on Ground With Daughter Kissing Her Forehead* [Image]. Unsplash. https://unsplash.com/photos/ElJfqMMBGUk

Chase, K. (2016). *Grayscale Photography of Child Beside Tree* [Image]. Unsplash. https://unsplash.com/photos/uNNvGTSwFtw

Darlami, K. (2021). *Woman in White and Black Floral Dress Carrying Baby* [Image]. Unsplash. https://unsplash.com/photos/iArVfiNwdQ0

De Silva, S. (2015). *Woman Wearing White Sweater Carrying a Daughter* [Image]. Unsplash. https://unsplash.com/photos/YLMs82LF6FY

Deluvio, C. (2020). *Person Sitting in a Chair in Front of a Man* [Image]. Unsplash. https://unsplash.com/photos/rRWiVQzLm7k

Dumlao, N. (2020). *Man in Black T-Shirt Holding Child in Gray Hoodie* [Image]. Unsplash. https://unsplash.com/photos/x-I4fs7i3WI

Gozalo, M. (2016). *Boy Playing Sand on Seashore During Sunset* [Image]. Unsplash. https://unsplash.com/photos/EcJhLyUQt2I

Hernandez, C. (2017). *Grayscale Photography of Two Girls Closing Their Mouths* [Image]. Unsplash. https://unsplash.com/photos/tJHU4mGSLz4

Krosky, K. (2018). *Woman Carrying Toddler Point at Hot Air Balloon* [Image]. Unsplash. https://unsplash.com/photos/2xjk8WWLFC4

Kulikova, K. (2021). *Man in White Dress Shirt and Woman in Brown Dress Standing on Green Grass Field During* [Image]. Unsplash. https://unsplash.com/photos/lSzARaEMbEU

Liebermann, J. (2018). *Man Carrying to Girls on Field of Red Petaled Flower* [Image]. Unsplash. https://unsplash.com/photos/O-RKu3Aqnsw

Makagonova, K. (2018). *Boy Sitting While Covering His Face* [Image]. Unsplash. https://unsplash.com/photos/9y6oH2qHai0

Muleba, H. (2019). *Smiling Man Carrying Child and Playing* [Image]. Unsplash. https://unsplash.com/photos/Cc-CQTUkbH0

Rockowitz, J. (2019). *Two Girls Lying on Woman Lap* [Image]. Unsplash. https://unsplash.com/photos/o0SkrZGvrKs

Spratt, A. (2018a). *Girl Reading Book on Bed* [Image]. Unsplash. https://unsplash.com/photos/hDcAjjkM-PU

Spratt, A. (2018b). *Two Person Near Trees* [Image]. Unsplash. https://unsplash.com/photos/yaX1QcPm2M8

Vistocco, M. (2018). *Man Holding Forehead Under Sunset* [Image]. Unsplash. https://unsplash.com/photos/CYN6x1FyPWs

Wheeler, J. (2018). *Woman Walking in Forest With Child* [Image]. Unsplash. https://unsplash.com/photos/RRZM3cwS1DU

www.ingramcontent.com/pod-product-compliance
Ingram Content Group UK Ltd.
Pitfield, Milton Keynes, MK11 3LW, UK
UKHW022023190726
13853UKWH00005B/2074